DATE DUE

THE JAMES SPRUNT STUDIES IN HISTORY AND POLITICAL SCIENCE

Published under the Direction of
the Departments of History and Political Science
of The University of North Carolina at Chapel Hill

VOLUME 49

Editors

HUGH TALMAGE LEFLER, CHAIRMAN

FEDERICO G. GIL

J. CARLYLE SITTERSON

KEENER C. FRAZER

GEORGE V. TAYLOR

THE PEACE PROPHETS

American Pacifist Thought, 1919-1941

By

John K. Nelson

CHAPEL HILL

THE UNIVERSITY OF NORTH CAROLINA PRESS

1967

Copyright © 1967 by
The University of North Carolina Press
Library of Congress Catalog Card Number: 67-65479
Manufactured in the United States of America

Printed by the Seeman Printery, Durham, N. C.

JX
1963
N35
1967

TO

MY MOTHER

AND IN MEMORY OF MY FATHER

PREFACE

These essays were originally prepared at a time when the Cold War appeared to have ended forever the possibility of American intellectuals paying any serious respect to pacifism. In the decade and a half from 1945 to 1960, few were prepared to question in a fundamental way the diplomatic and defensive strategies of the Cold War. American policy was not only defended as a necessity but also heralded as a coming of age for the United States, as a realization at long last of maturity. From the perspective of those tense and troubled days, the pre-war flirtation with pacifism appeared as quaint and irresponsible, a final expression of the nation's reluctance to grow up.

Once again, however, with the "thaw" in East-West relations, with the public concern and confusion attending American involvement in the Vietnam war, and with the moral sensitivity engendered by the civil-rights movement, pacifism has reared its head. Its appeal to a new generation of radical dissent, both as a general philosophy of life and as a specific technique for effecting social and economic reform, is apparent. In reality, as these essays show, this contemporary attraction to nonviolence and nonviolent resistance is less a discovery than a rediscovery. Dissent in the 1920's and 1930's had its encounter too with pacifism and celebrated Gandhi as the prophet of a new era in human relations. No portrayal of the ideals and aspirations of the American people would be faithful or complete without some attention paid to the recurring minor theme of pacifism.

This study makes no pretense to definitiveness. It describes the pacifist response to immediate concerns and circumstances as reflected in the periodical literature of the period. The pacifists who expressed themselves through this medium represented only a segment of the movement, a vigorous and articulate segment consisting largely of recent converts drawn principally from the ranks of Protestant clergymen and theologians and of political commentators and journalists of liberal and radical leanings. The study does not have in view the sober second thoughts or more ambitious systematic defenses of the pacifist position but rather the more instant responses in analysis and proposal. Following a brief survey of its sources and historical development consideration is given to the three major problems confronting pacifists in the inter-war period: the understanding of war and conflict, the relevance of pacifism to the search for economic and social justice, and the formulation of a program for a stable international order.

Frank W. Klingberg, Fletcher M. Green, Hugh T. Lefler, and the late James E. King gave freely, not only of time, counsel, and critical discernment, but also of encouragement. First as a student and then as a colleague, I have been immeasurably enriched by my association with them. I am particularly grateful to the staff of the University of North Carolina Library for easing the tasks of research and to the editors of the James Sprunt Studies in History and Political Science for their generous aid in the preparation of this volume.

J.K.N.

Chapel Hill, North Carolina
March, 1967

CONTENTS

THE PEACE PROPHETS

CHAPTER I

PACIFISM AND PACIFISTS: AN INTRODUCTION

"Pacifism," said the Very Reverend Robert I. Gannon, president of Fordham University, "is to the true love of peace what prohibition is to temperance. It is the image of virtue distorted by heresy."[1] Many Americans in the twenties and the thirties regarded pacifism as a ". . . pink-tearish apology for cowardice . . . ;"[2] they saw the pacifists as consorting with Communists and anarchists. Not only was pacifism a term of disdain, it was also uncritically applied to groups varying widely on the political spectrum: isolationists, socialists, and even pro-Nazi sympathizers. The term "pacifism," coming nearer the mark, was generally used to designate those actively working for peace. Here too, however, the term lacked precision because the peace groups had such greatly divergent aims.

For the purposes of this study, pacifism is defined as ". . . the renunciation on moral grounds of offensive or defensive military action."[3] George Hartmann, a Columbia University psychologist, in preparing a test of the motivational differences between pacifists and non-pacifists defined the former as ". . . absolute and unconditional resisters to war in any form. . . ."[4] Pacifism was carefully distinguished from internationalism by Norman Angell; it was most meaningfully comprehended, he wrote, as ". . . the doctrine of those who refuse to sanction war for any purpose, defensive or otherwise, in contradistinction to the views of internationalists who would serve peace by international organization, and who would either take no stand on the question of military restraint or advocate placing it under the control of an international agency."[5]

To stop short with this definition would be to leave the forcible impression of negativeness or passivity which the modern pacifist has tried with self-conscious exertions to overcome. He insists that pacifism is a positive philosophy of life, a revolutionary mode of ordering all

[1] *The New Republic,* LXXXIX (December 16, 1936), 219.

[2] Ernest L. Meyer, "A Pacifist Defends the Legion," *The Christian Century,* XLIV (November 9, 1932), 1373.

[3] *Subject Headings Used in the Dictionary Catalogues of the Library of Congress.* Edited by Nella Jane Martin. Fifth Edition (Washington: Library of Congress, 1948), p. 805.

[4] George W. Hartmann, "Motivational Differences Between Pacifists and Non-Pacifists," *The Journal of Social Psychology,* XIV (August, 1941), 198.

[5] Norman Angell, "Pacifism," *Encyclopaedia of the Social Sciences,* 15 volumes. Edited by Edwin R. A. Seligman and Alvin Johnson (New York: The Macmillan Company, 1930-1935), XI, 527.

human relationships.[6] The strongest, most vital, and enduring source of pacifism in the Western world has been the conviction that the Christian injunction to love implies non-violence in all the relationships of life as well. It is "the way of the Cross,"[7] the path of "sacrificial suffering,"[8] or ". . . the entire attitude . . . of one who has renounced hatred."[9] Implicit in these phrases is the belief in the sanctity of human personality, a value that supercedes all human formulations of goals and values.

The positive character of pacifism arises from its identification with a spiritual attitude toward life as conceptualized in such expressions as "trust," "good will," "cooperation," and "love." This attitude when active in the affairs of men is believed to possess a force or power superior to physical violence or coercion. Thus John Haynes Holmes argued that pacifism, far from being untested, has already proved itself triumphant in the daily relationships of individuals. It is ironic, he thought, that ". . . the very men who accept force and violence as the divinely-ordained method of controlling and directing human affairs, are most of them exemplifying in their personal relations the program of pure pacifism."[10] The task of the religious pacifist was to show men that the bonds of trust and good will evident in family relationships were relevant to the ordering of economic, social, and political life both on the national and the international scene.

Allied to this is a faith in the individual conscience, an independence of the person from the edicts of the state where they infringe upon his moral and spiritual convictions. This faith, no doubt, is the product not alone of the respect for human personality, but of the historical experience of persecution and disdain withstood by pacifists in maintaining

[6] The difficulty in defining and understanding the nature of pacifism is confirmed by a study conducted by George Hartmann, a Columbia University psychologist. In his analysis of the replies of seventy-five of the most notable philosophers and teachers of philosophy in the United States to his questionnaire sent out in 1942 requesting these men to state the best argument *for* and *against* pacifism, Hartmann concludes, "The indecisive nature of the separate points reflects the unsatisfactory state of thinking in the area. . . ." (140). A reading of the replies which are reproduced in the article will confirm his judgment that here is an area of thought practically left untouched by philosophers. Hartmann's final conclusion is that the arguments offered for pacifism seem to be the stronger ones. George W. Hartmann, "The Strength and Weakness of the Pacifist Position As Seen by American Philosophers," *The Philosophical Review,* LIII (March, 1944), 125-144.

[7] Ernest Fremont Tittle, "If America Is Drawn into War, Can You, As a Christian, Participate in It or Support It?" *The Christian Century,* LVIII (February 5, 1941), 179.

[8] Albert Wentworth Palmer, "If America Is Drawn into War, Can You, As a Christian, Participate in It or Support It?" *The Christian Century,* LVIII (January 8, 1941), 52.

[9] David Elton Trueblood, "The Renunciation of Hatred," *The Christian Century,* LIII (April 15, 1936), 564.

[10] John Haynes Holmes, "Pacifism in Personal Relations," *The World Tomorrow,* XI (December, 1928), 511.

the testimony of peace throughout the seemingly endless succession of wars. Many pacifists have also tended to exemplify the ideal of the simple life. This is most true of the quietist sects which have sought to live in terms of a literal interpretation of the Sermon on the Mount but the concept has become so interwoven with pacifism that it has even permeated a modern definition by a revolutionary socialist.[11] Religious pacifism thus is far from being the simple renunciation of international conflict. It is best understood as an approach to life, as a complex pattern of ideas evolved from belief and historical experience. The religious pacifist is an idealist who ". . . in the face of hatred and war puts to the test of action the faith that the nature of God as universal love makes certain that evil must yield to good."[12]

Closely allied to the religious pacifist is the individual who arrives at pacifism by the avenue of ethical judgment. His beliefs, while stripped of the religious imagery, center upon identical concepts of the worth of human personality and the destructiveness of violence or force. His idealism is bound up as well in the absolute value of truth, peace, and love.

Another source of modern pacifism has been the rationalistic calculation of the nature and consequences of war. A revulsion at the negation of humane values and the democratic faith has led the rationalist to his anti-war protest. Political and philosophical liberals have seen in war the abnegation of human integrity, the antithesis of progress, the doom of individualism. The utilitarian has added up the cost in dollars and cents and has compiled horrendous tables of the dead, wounded, and missing in his indictment of war as a means of resolving international discord. Thus war itself has been a potent breeder of pacifism. The variety of approaches to pacifism should make evident the complexity of pacifism as an idea and as a mode of action—a complexity that becomes more entangled as the forms of American pacifist thought are examined.

The sources of pacifism in the American experience have been primarily religious; yet the expressions of pacifism, like the atomistic propensity of the American church, have been diverse. Pacifists have united in their opposition to international war; but a deeper question, implicit in their opposition to war, has been the source of profound differences. These differences became evident when the pacifists proceeded to explain what it was about war to which they objected. Was it

[11] Ammon A. Hennacy, "Inside or Outside? Two Views on the Relation of Pacifists to Revolutionary Movements. I. Working Inside," *The World Tomorrow,* VII (July, 1924), 201.

[12] "Christian Pacifists Take Their Stand," *The Christian Century,* LVI (March 15, 1939), 344.

the mass physical violence unrestrained by law, or the use of force itself in any form? The writings of the pacifists provide a treasure store for the enterprising semanticist because much of this debate is obscured in the ambiguities of undefined words and phrases, and in the desire of each writer to provide his unique contribution to the delineation of the good and evil involved in the use, or the refusal to use, force.

At the one end of the no-force to absolute force polarity is a body of thought that is best termed "nonresistance." This is the historic pacifism of such Christian sects as the Albigenses, Waldenses, Lollards, Hussites, Dukhobors, and Moravians. Though modern Protestant exponents of the social gospel would dissent vigorously, careful scholars such as C. J. Cadoux and H. Richard Niebuhr believe that "nonresistance" best describes the attitude and actions of Jesus and of the way of life of his followers in the first centuries of the Christian era.[13] Nonresistance has been preached in the United States by the quietist sects: the Brethren, some groups of the Quakers, and, with particular faithfulness even in the present day, the Mennonites. A look at Mennonite doctrine reveals the characteristics of this area of pacifist thought.

The Mennonites believe that the use of force or coercion, whether physical or mental, is evil. This belief arises from a literal interpretation of the Scriptures. The Ten Commandments of the Old Testament reveal the fundamental law of God for all men in all time, but God, by a "covenant" with the people of the Old Testament, mitigated the demands of this fundamental law because of the lower state of the pre-Christian moral consciousness. The exemptions were embodied in the Mosaic civil law which governed the Jews until the time of Jesus when a "new covenant" was made. By its provisions men to this day are held accountable for a strict observance of the fundamental law because they have been shown the way to fulfill it by the deeds and teachings of Jesus. Nonresistance thus embodies more than an obedience to the Sixth Commandment; it envisions a life lived in consonance with the Sermon on the Mount with its call to ". . . resist not evil, but whoever shall smite thee on they right cheek, turn to him the other also. . . . Love your enemies, bless them that curse you, do good to them that hate you. . . ."[14] The Mennonites have no fond vision that this expression of life as love is going to establish on this earth a perfect kingdom, or a just social order. They are otherworldly, fundamentalist

[13] C. J. Cadoux, "The Christian Pacifist Case," *The Journal of Religion,* XXI (July, 1941), 235; H. Richard Niebuhr, "The Grace of Doing Nothing," *The Christian Century,* XLIX (March 23, 1932), 374. For a provocative and thorough analysis of religious pacifism treated in terms of the sociological concepts developed by Ernst Troeltsch and Max Weber see David A. Martin, *Pacifism: An Historical and Sociological Study* (New York: Schocken Books, 1966. Hereinafter cited as Martin, *Pacifism.*)

[14] St. Matthew 5: 39-44.

in their theology, living as patient pilgrims awaiting the reign of peace in another world.

This denial of force itself has meant that the Mennonites refuse to participate in any activity of the civil authority that involves the use of force; they conceive of themselves as a Christian brotherhood apart from the state which they recognize as a necessary expression of force for the maintenance of order and the administration of justice in an evil society. The Mennonites hold, for example, that it is better to suffer injustice than to take a legal matter into the courts, for civil and criminal law rests on the implicit, if not explicit, use of force. Love, not justice, is the true aim of the Christian life. Nevertheless, the Mennonites believe in submission to the laws of the state except when they encroach on matters of faith or morals. At that point, they assert the historic doctrine of the separation of church and state. Interpreting this doctrine in its literal sense, the Mennonites have achieved a separation of church and state distinct from other religious bodies in the United States. The means of sustaining the separation has been the rural community where Mennonites have separated themselves from society as well. They have not ignored suffering in human society, however, for they have adopted a program of world-wide relief similar to that carried on by the Quakers.[15]

The element of anarchy inherent in nonresistance is more apparent in the thought of two nineteenth century figures who adopted nonresistance as their philosophy of life: William Lloyd Garrison and Leo Tolstoy. Both have exerted a considerable influence on contemporary pacifist thought, though nonresistance has been consistently held to by only a few individuals and the quietist sects.

The quietism of the Quakers is quite another matter. Growing up in the century following the Reformation and maturing in the age of the Enlightenment, Quaker thought has been receptive to winds of optimism, rationalism, and humanism. Consequently its pacifism has a flavor distinct from that of the Mennonites, a divergence accelerated during the nineteenth century. It is difficult to express the exact nature of the difference; it is more a reflection of a different view of the world and of the nature of man. It is also a little dangerous to essay the task of describing Quaker thought; its resistance to theological formulation, its noncreedal position, and the many areas of disagreement among Quakers make possible only a statement of general principles that have characterized its life and thought down to our time.

The Friends have been primarily interested in religious experience

[15] This description of Mennonite life and thought is drawn from Guy Franklin Hershberger, *War, Peace, and Nonresistance* (Scottsdale, Pennsylvania: The Herald Press, 1946), *passim.* (Hereinafter cited as Hershberger, *War, Peace, and Nonresistance.*)

rather than theology. They have historically been more concerned with the actuality of everyday relationships between man and man, and man and God, than in the theory of the nature of these relationships. Yet their actions and thoughts have revealed definite conceptions of the meaning of these relationships. God is conceived of as the Father, as the "one eternal loving Spirit."[16] In contrast to the Mennonites, who regard man as a sinful being, the Quakers tend to see him as a rational creature "akin" to the nature of God because the seed of God is planted within him. The meeting between God and man takes place not through the offices of the Church or the mysteries of the sacraments but through the "inner light"—a direct illumination of God in man's inner being or conscience. It is this "light" rather than any external authority which is the guide to human conduct. By considering men as potential sons of God—potential because the living presence of Christ is available to all men as a source of wisdom and a guide for conduct—the Quakers discern the world about them not as inherently evil but as a field for the creation of the Kingdom of God, for the realization of a just social order. Thus the failure of man to achieve goodness and happiness can be attributed to defects in society which man through the spiritual resources available to him and through his wisdom and diligence can eradicate. The Quaker therefore singles out problems or evils in society and sets about to reform and remake them in terms of the Kingdom ideal.

In the nineteenth century it was slavery which, in particular, aroused the moral abhorrence of the Quakers. Unlike the Mennonites, who accepted slavery as a part of an evil world, the Quakers waged an unceasing war to do away with this cancer in American society. In doing so the Quakers accepted the state as the necessary means of ordering human life and securing justice. They have come to modify in three important ways the nonresistance of the Mennonites. Because they have accepted the world as the site for the creation of a just social order, love and good will have become much more than a literal obedience to scriptural commands, they have become the means or method of creating the new society; in fact, they have become a form of force itself.

By accepting the goal of the Kingdom on earth, the Quakers have been forced to define the specific evils and obstructions in the present world that are hindering progress toward the ideal. Thus they have become the opponents not only of war, but of all forms of oppression. By setting themselves in opposition both to the violence of war and the varied forms of oppression in society they have given rise to a tension that must eternally dog modern pacifists. Their goal is no longer

[16] David Elton Trueblood, "The Renunciation of Hatred," *The Christian Century,* LIII (April 15, 1936), 563.

simply peace—in the sense of the absence of war or violence—but a new social order which means that the temptation is always present to sacrifice the purity of the means, defined *a priori* as love and good will, to achieve the goal when some speedier or seemingly more effective method offers itself. Thus non-violent love which is both the ideal end and the practical means for the Quaker becomes constantly subjected to questioning and doubt.

Finally, by accepting the state and, consequently, the force necessary to sustain it, the Quakers have rejected the definition of all force as evil and have set about on the more difficult task of defining precisely the modes of force or coercion to which they object. They have most often answered this by defining physical violence as evil. They have further qualified this position by distinguishing between physical coercion as exercised by the domestic police force under a system of law and the lawless physical violence of war. The problem of defining good and evil means of force becomes less susceptible of solution the more it is discussed because its implications are so infinite and intricate. The conflict between means and ends aroused by this development in Quaker pacifism has perplexed pacifists especially in the twentieth century. The Quakers on the whole have remained faithful to their testimony both against the war system and against oppression in the social order. They have maintained their devotion to peace in the face of these tensions and doubts and have contributed the form of pacifism most widely held in the nineteenth and twentieth centuries—non-violent resistance.

Non-violent resistance, the ". . . faith in the creative and conquering power of love as a method of life with our fellows,"[17] carries the appeal of an imperative to action; it seeks to abolish war through social action, education, and spiritual discipline. The Quakers, reasoning that every man partakes in some measure of the nature of God, believe that the way to bring about understanding and peace is to treat men so as to draw out these qualities in their natures. The problem is seen as that of guiding individuals to this way of life, for if only enough people would accept it, no nation could wage war. The idea and example of Quaker pacifism have had a deep attraction for men who have found war to be the supreme evil and yet who have desired to remain in a positive relation to the world about them. It led Harry Emerson Fosdick to remark. ". . . I am essentially a Quaker . . .";[18] Albert Palmer declared that he

[17] Rufus Matthew Jones, *The Faith and Practice of the Quakers.* Seventh Edition (London: Methuen and Company, 1949), p. 165. (Hereinafter cited as Jones, *Quakers.*)

[18] Harry Emerson Fosdick, "If America Is Drawn into War, Can You, As a Christian, Participate in It or Support It?" *The Christian Century,* LVIII (January 22, 1941), 118.

was moving irresistibly to the Quaker position in the trying months preceding Pearl Harbor.[19]

Non-violent resistance attracted the great influx of liberal Protestant ministers into the pacifist ranks following the First World War. The vast destruction of the war, the terrifying inhumanity of the weapons of war devised by modern science, and the growing awareness of the interdependent nature of the world elevated peace to the first position in their hierarchy of goals for the achievement of a new society. By the end of the twenties a mounting sense of crisis swept their ranks as the international peace structure erected by the victors at Versailles appeared fatally inadequate to meet the challenge of a world faced with economic disaster and threats of aggression. Norman Thomas wrote, "It is this psychological attitude, this predisposition to a kind of collective suicide, which makes the future so dark. . . ."[20]

This urgency and the intellectual dominance of these new concepts produced a subtle change in the emphasis of the pacifism of the period. It came to be regarded more as a means or a technique to achieve social ends than as the attitude or way of life. The goal was the reconstruction of the political and economic order both within and among nations. This appeared as an overwhelming but, nevertheless, urgent task, for the pacifists had awakened to the realization that war has its roots in nationalism and economic imperialism. Looking about, the pacifists found stirring examples of the power of non-violent resistance to effect social change though they persistently exaggerated the significance of the events they cited. The labor strike when kept within peaceful bounds had won momentous victories. China employed a boycott against Great Britain in 1925-1926; the German people by peaceful resistance defeated the Kapp *putsch* in Berlin in 1920, and for a considerable period of time rendered the French occupation of the Ruhr a veritable nightmare to the French economy.[21] The pacifists probed their history books to find reassuring examples of non-violent resistance in the Deak revolt in Hungary in 1866,[22] in the successful resistance of the Bahaists to

[19] Albert Wentworth Palmer, "If America Is Drawn into War, Can You, As a Christian, Participate in It or Support It?" *The Christian Century,* LVIII (January 8, 1941), 52. The material on Quakerism and Quaker pacifism is drawn from Jones, *Quakers, passim;* David Elton Trueblood, "The Renunciation of Hatred," *The Christian Century,* LIII (April 15, 1936), 563-564; David Elton Trueblood, "The Quaker Way," *The Atlantic Monthly,* CLXVI (December, 1940), 740-746.

[20] Norman Thomas, "What About the Use of Violence?" *The World Tomorrow,* XV (April 1, 1932), 105.

[21] John Nevin Sayre, "Pacifism and National Security," *The World Tomorrow,* XI (August, 1928), 333.

[22] G. C. Field presents a strong criticism of this incident as an example of non-violent resistance. He points out that Austria was weak because of her recent defeat at Sadowa and that immediately after the Deak revolt the Hungarians offered themselves as soldiers to fight on the side of Austria against her external

Turkish persecution, and in the civil disobedience of the Underground Railroad. But the pervading influence in this mounting interest in non-violent means of effecting social change was the dynamic figure of Gandhi. A flood of books and magazine articles during the twenties and thirties kept constantly before the public the remarkable fight of the Indian against the British Empire. Pacifists began to speak of the "Gandhian method," "non-violent coercion," "soul-force," and "non-violent non-cooperation." Gandhi was the symbol as well as the justification of the relevance of this method to the solution of social problems. Pacifist writers became interested in explaining the wide range of tactics available to them in the acceptance of the Gandhian form of pacifism. Devere Allen saw three modes of action available to American pacifist strategists: non-violent resistance in the event of a hostile invasion or act of aggression; non-violent attack to effect the elimination of injustice in civil and social situations; and non-violent mass action to prevent a nation from going to war.[23] Gandhi's example was pervasive. He ". . . stimulated groups like the Mennonites to restate their counter doctrine of nonresistance . . . ;" he ". . . furnished much of the inspiration for the abstract theory of pacifism, as well as the stimulus for such actions as hunger strikes, work strikes, protests, and civil disobedience . . . ,"[24] and, finally, he forced a thorough-going consideration of the problem of coercion.

Some pacifists entered strong protests against this new concern with strategy and tactics. The "Gandhi method," they pointed out, was but another form of warfare. Guy Hershberger, a Mennonite, contended that ". . . the primary objective of nonviolence is not peace, or obedience to the divine will, but rather certain desired social changes for personal, or class, or national advantages. . . . When Jesus said, 'Love your enemies,' He did not mean by this: love your enemies to make them do you good."[25] Umphrey Lee agreed that nonviolence was ". . . still a technique for overcoming a superior force, and has little more relation to the teachings of Jesus than the technique of war."[26] But these

---

foes. G. C. Field, *Pacifism and the Conscientious Objector* (Cambridge: Cambridge University Press, 1945), pp. 28-29.

[23] Devere Allen, *The Fight for Peace* (New York: The Macmillan Company, 1940), p. 623. (Hereinafter cited as Allen, *Fight for Peace.*)

[24] Mulford Q. Sibley and Philip E. Jacob, *Conscription of Conscience: The American State and the Conscientious Objector, 1940-1947* (Ithaca: Cornell University Press, 1952), p. 40. (Hereinafter cited as Sibley and Jacob, *Conscription.*) An influential popular exposition of the Gandhian position was first published in 1934, and subsequently revised and reprinted several times, by Richard B. Gregg, *The Power of Nonviolence* (Nyack, New York: Fellowship Publications, 1959.)

[25] Hershberger, *War, Peace, and Nonresistance,* pp. 1, 225, 279.

[26] Umphrey Lee, *The Historic Church and Modern Pacifism* (New York: Abingdon-Cokesbury Press, 1943), p. 217. (Hereinafter cited as Lee, *Historic Church.*)

objections could do little to diminish the enthusiasm of those who saw the bright possibilities of remaking the world. Peace still conceived to be the ultimate goal was made dependent on an array of other goals to be achieved first: the end to economic exploitation both by nations and classes, the achievement of social equality, the termination of racial and national prejudices, the fight on militarism and imperialism, and the reform of the penal system. American Socialists saw in Gandhian pacifism an alternative to the doctrine of democratic gradualism; a way in which the class revolution could come about peacefully through the use of strikes, boycotts, and civil disobedience.

As the pacifists of the inter-war period turned to the problem of force, they began to talk like social technocrats. Force emerged as the central concern for which they perfected an elaborate calculus to determine the proper course of action. Gone was the blissful simplicity of the Mennonite dictum that all force is evil. The new orientation appeared more realistic to be sure; yet it opened the door to endless doubts and a score of possible heresies. One thing the pacifists could agree upon: international war was evil because it destroyed the innocent with the guilty; it aggravated rather than settled the disputes over which the war was begun; and it was used by the parties to the dispute without benefit of law or an impartial authority to render judgment. However, pacifists began to argue that not only were force and conflict necessary in society but that they were creative. Harold Bosley demonstrated, to his own satisfaction at least, that the conflict between ideas, desires, and instincts was a good thing as was the conflict between political parties and between the elements of convention and innovation.[27] All human relationships were involved in some measure of force and coercion. The state collected taxes, protected health, and administered justice with the use of force. In the family, force played a redemptive role by teaching restraint and discipline.

Thus another means of evaluating force was needed, and the pacifists met the dilemma by formulating some rough-hewn rules of thumb. Kirby Page believed the test was whether or not force served or violated the "family spirit."[28] Seeing that there was no wholly satisfactory method of action, the form of coercion to be used, he concluded, must be the one that involved the minimum of suffering and the maximum of redemption.[29] Reinhold Niebuhr agreed with this pragmatic rule of action, substituting the test of a minimum of destruction for that of suffering.[30]

[27] Harold Bosley, "Illusions of the Disillusioned," *The Christian Century,* LVIII (January 1, 1941), 14.

[28] Kirby Page, "Is Coercion Ever Justifiable?" *The World Tomorrow,* XV (June, 1932), 173.

[29] *Ibid.,* 174.

[30] Reinhold Niebuhr, "Pacifism and the Use of Force," *The World Tomorrow,* XI (May, 1928), 219.

The criterion might be restated as an estimation of the potential effects on human personality. Page observed that ". . . there is no inherent irreconcilability between love and coercion, but rather the reverse, under some circumstances love ceases to be love if it fails to use moral means of restraint."[31] Page discovered in the life of Jesus—" . . . a burning denunciation of iniquity and an indomitable resistance to evil."[32] The pacifists had moved far from the gentle quietism of the Mennonites and the Quakers.

Most new pacifists of the inter-war period found that they could accept the domestic police force but with reservations; they felt an ethical distinction must be established between coercion and killing, imprisonment and electrocution. Similarly some discerned a meaningful distinction between international non-military sanctions and armed hostilities, and between economic-political compulsion and violent class war.[33] These judgments offered no real challenge to the Quaker distinction between force and violence. The challenge to traditional pacifism came from the intent to use the method of non-violent resistance as a tool or weapon to effect changes in the economic and political order. This new thought was but one step away from an idea which would disrupt the fundamental nature of pacifism. That step would seem to have been taken by George Coe when he stated that ". . . the use of force, physical and mechanical, is unavoidable, whatever our plans and purposes; that the ethically justified scope of force is not restricted to what is commanded or permitted by law; that the test for all employment of force is its observed effect in opportunities and incentives for growth of persons and for fellowship and cooperation; and that, finally, the danger that is in the doctrine is inherent in personal life as such. . . ."[34] Coe implied that if a pragmatic test in terms of the effect on personality could be applied to the use of non-violent forms of coercion, the same test could be applied to mechanical and physical forms of coercion as well.

A close examination of the life of Gandhi seemed to indicate similar finely-drawn distinctions. The Indian reformer served with the British army as a noncombatant in both the Boer War and the First World War so that he might have some claim on the British for a better role for India within the Commonwealth. At the same time that he was preaching the renunciation of war to the Western nations, he sought for

[31] Kirby Page, "Is Coercion Compatible with Religion?" *The World Tomorrow,* XVI (March 1, 1933), 211.

[32] Kirby Page, "Is Coercion Ever Justifiable?" *The World Tomorrow,* XV (June, 1932), 173.

[33] Kirby Page, "Class War and Religion," *The World Tomorrow,* XVI (March 8, 1933), 226.

[34] George Albert Coe, "What Is Violence?" *The World Tomorrow,* XV (October 19, 1932), 380.

India the right to control her own defensive forces.[35] The basic tension implicit in modern pacifism was nowhere better exemplified than in these acts and teachings of Gandhi. His consuming ambition in life was a political one—that of achieving political independence for India—yet he was an adherent of non-violence and the belief in the triumph of good over evil by the ways of love and good will as taught by the great religious teachers of all times.

The tension facing the pacifists with the rise of totalitarian dictatorships and with the increasing desire to work actively for a just economic order in the United States was rarely acknowledged openly. The pacifists evolved a tenuous compromise between the Quaker peace idealism and the Gandhian non-violent technique of social warfare. They created an image or vision of a vast effort on the part of people the world over uniting to bring in the Kingdom both of peace and justice. It is only by an understanding of these two parallel, and sometimes conflicting, trends in pacifist thought that one can understand Bishop Paul Jones's definition of pacifism as ". . . an attitude to life arising from a belief in human capacity for social action, which stresses the importance of the reaction of person upon person and group upon group, and which consequently uses only methods calculated to evoke co-operative action in seeking to achieve a progressive integration of life in every field of human relations . . . ," and seeks ". . . to reorganize our social machinery so as to draw upon the cooperative and friendly capacity of human beings. . . ."[36] The latter statement, a seemingly uncalculated inversion of the Quaker ideal, was at one and the same time the distinctive achievement of pacifist thought and the source of its most profound dilemma when faced with the necessity to act.

Merle Curti has called the peace movement in the United States "a story of tragedy."[37] It has also been the story of a remarkably sustained testimony against war and a rich drama of vigorous and skillful leadership in the face of public apathy and antipathy. Pacifism has been preached in this country ever since colonial days when the first Quakers, Brethren, and Mennonites migrated to the New World. The "holy experiment" of William Penn in government and in Indian relations continues to provide pacifists with a justification of the applicability of non-violent means to the affairs of state. To the United States belongs the distinction of having given rise to the first organized peace societies

[35] Bartholomew De Ligt, "Mahatma Gandhi's Attitude Toward War," *The World Tomorrow,* XV (March, 1932), 75-76.

[36] Paul Jones, "The Meaning of Pacifism," *The World Tomorrow,* XI (April, 1928), 162, 163.

[37] Merle Curti, *Peace or War: The American Struggle 1636-1936* (New York: W. W. Norton and Company, 1936), p. 13. (Hereinafter cited as Curti, *Peace or War.*)

in modern times, perhaps in all of man's history. In 1815 three such societies were organized independently in various parts of the country. The first was founded by David Low Dodge in New York City in August, 1815. A group of Friends in Vienna, Ohio, established the second; the third, the Massachusetts Peace Society, was organized in the home of William Ellery Channing under the leadership of Noah Worcester in December, 1815.[38] By 1828, the year of the founding of the American Peace Society, there were over thirty societies in the United States.[39] The movement by this time had spread to or arisen independently in England, France, and Switzerland. Ten years later, in 1838, William Lloyd Garrison formed the New England Nonresistance Society, a specifically pacifist group which even challenged the very concept of government. In 1846 Elihu Burritt fashioned his League of Universal Brotherhood and by his diligence and zeal persuaded over forty thousand persons to sign a personal pacifist pledge.[40]

The pre-Civil War period may be characterized in several ways. It was a time of intelligent, skillful leadership both by moderates such as Noah Worcester[41] and by radical pacifists such as William Ladd, whose famous "Essay on a Congress of Nations" in 1840 envisioned a world court and a world legislature, David Low Dodge, Theodore Grimké, William Lloyd Garrison, who exerted a deep influence on the thought of Tolstoy (who, interestingly enough, was a source of inspiration to Gandhi), and, finally, Elihu Burritt, best remembered as the "Learned Blacksmith" who conceived the idea of international peace congresses to press for arbitration and the codification of international law. The vigor of their thought was remarkable. Devere Allen has contended that ". . . the ideology and tactics of 1834 are separated by an astonishingly slender margin from the ideology and tactics of today."[42]

The pacifist movement, apart from the peace churches, was then, as it has been throughout its history, primarily a middle-class movement led by the clergy and a few responsive laymen.[43] It has had comparatively little appeal to the general populace and but a small measure of influence in government. The coming of the Civil War revealed another pattern that was to remain true throughout the course of the history of the peace movement. Except for a handful of the members of the peace societies and the faithfulness of the peace churches, the peace lovers rushed to support the war. The societies either collapsed or struggled on near the verge of extinction. Elihu Burritt was one of the few leaders who remained true to his pledge in 1861. But with the signing

38 Allen, *Fight for Peace,* p. 4.
39 *Ibid.,* p. 11.
40 Curti, *Peace or War,* p. 38.
41 Allen, *Fight for Peace,* p. 9.
42 *Ibid.,* p. 384.
43 Curti, *Peace or War,* p. 13.

of the peace the movement came to life once again with renewed strength.

Hope pervaded the peace movement from 1865 to 1914. Despite the unsettling imperialist adventures in the Caribbean and the Pacific, vigorous efforts to erect a peace structure seemed blessed with success on every side until the catastrophe of the summer of 1914 revealed the flimsiness and shallowness of these confident expectations. In 1866 a federation of peace societies created the Universal Peace Union under the leadership of Alfred Love, a well-to-do Philadelphia wool merchant. Love, a forceful pacifist leader, developed the use of symbols and slogans to add color and appeal to the peace message—a task that has continually baffled peace lovers for war, by some fateful decree, lends itself to drama and excitement while peace has an anemic, nebulous quality that poses a mighty challenge to the propagandist.[44] Love paid his respects to the other reform movements of the day by accepting both women and Negroes on a basis of equality into the Union.

Arbitration was deemed to be the road to peace by this generation of peace makers. Their agitation led to a renewal of international peace conferences beginning in 1889 and continuing until 1913, a series that met in the principal cities of Europe and the United States in all but five of the years during this span of time. Many pacifists were severely critical of these conferences, describing them as tame, conservative affairs more interested in winning the applause and endorsement of world political leaders than in dealing with the complexities of a world plagued with the curse of war.[45]

The Spanish American War, while momentarily disrupting the campaign for peace, attracted a host of anti-imperialist liberals, led by William Jennings Bryan, into the peace ranks and brought a renewal of conferences aimed primarily at obtaining acceptance of the principle of arbitration by the nations of the world. The fruit of these efforts were the Hague Conferences of 1899 and 1907 and the establishment in 1907 of the Permanent Court of Arbitration. The forceful impact of the arbitration idea so long advocated by conservative peace societies was evident in the efforts of Elihu Root and William Jennings Bryan to conclude treaties of arbitration and conciliation.

The opening decades of the twentieth century also witnessed the formation of two great peace societies: Edwin Ginn's World Peace Foundation, founded in Boston in 1910, and Andrew Carnegie's Carnegie Endowment for International Peace established in the same year in New York. These were well-managed peace corporations directing highly successful programs of peace propaganda and education, but again to rigorous pacifists they seemed hopelessly conservative and

[44] *Ibid.*, p. 79.
[45] Allen, *Fight for Peace*, p. 481.

respectable. Of the World Peace Foundation one wrote, ". . . the spirit eulogized by Edwin Ginn has been as alien to the organization as the great comet that lighted the skies in celebration of his princely gift."[46] Significant as well during the period were the formation in 1904 of the Intercollegiate Peace Association at Goshen College, a Mennonite school in Indiana,[47] and the founding of the Church Peace Union on the eve of the First World War, again a demonstration of the endeavors of Andrew Carnegie to bring the world a step closer to peace.

The period from 1865 to 1914 witnessed a growth of the peace churches in numbers and influence. In 1867 the Peace Association of Friends began its long and faithful career. The seventies witnessed the immigration of Mennonites and Hutterites from Germany and Russia. It was these peace sects and a few members of the Universal Peace Union who alone withstood Wilson's magnetic call for a Great Crusade to end war for all time. The peace foundations and the Church Peace Union vigorously endorsed the government, and prominent peace leaders assumed important roles in the prosecution of the war effort.

The shock and disrupture caused by previous wars to the peace movement were as nothing compared to the experience of the First World War. Yet out of this traumatic experience and the subsequent disillusionment with the failure of the Versailles Treaty, came the most vigorous peace movement in American history and a decided trend toward radical pacifism: "Never in world history was peace so great a desideratum, so much talked about, looked toward, and planned for, as in the decade after the 1918 Armistice."[48] Quincy Wright, drawing upon his magisterial study of warfare, observed that ". . . during the life of a civilization there has been a tendency for very severe war periods to be followed by movements for peace."[49] Sensitive, influential intellectual and religious leaders joined pacifist organizations because they saw through the dark-tinted glasses of the twenties ". . . the antiquated senility of war on the one hand and the quavering instability of the improvised organization of peace on the other."[50] *The Christian Century,* looking back from the vantage point of 1939, commented that in no comparable span of time ". . . have such widespread, persistent, and intelligent efforts been put forth to establish peace on a firm foundation

[46] *Ibid.,* 507.

[47] Curti, *Peace or War,* p. 212.

[48] Robert H. Ferrell, *Peace in Their Time: The Origins of the Kellogg-Briand Pact* (New Haven: Yale University Press, 1952), p. 14. (Hereinafter cited as Ferrell, *Peace in Their Time.*)

[49] Quincy Wright, *A Study of War,* 2 volumes (Chicago: University of Chicago Press, 1942), I, 384.

[50] Halford Edward Luccock, "Religion and World Crisis," *The World Tomorrow,* XIV (November, 1931), 365.

as during these two decades."[51] Despite the frantic desire for peace the pacifist was still generally regarded as *persona non grata* by the public; ". . . it seems the grimmest joke of the ages," *The New Republic* declared, "that 'pacifism' is still a thoroughly unpopular doctrine and that any man who tries to warn the people of their danger is more than likely to be laughed out of court."[52]

The conservative peace societies and foundations continued their program of education, research, and propaganda. These groups could point to solid accomplishments during the period. Supported by the pacifists, they performed yeoman's service in arousing public opinion on behalf of the Washington Conference of 1921-1922. They so successfully denounced the War Department's Mobilization Day in 1924 that the idea was dropped in 1925. In the realm of international affairs they exerted every effort to prevent the outbreak of war with Mexico in 1924 and to direct the weight of public opinion against further meddling in the affairs of China. The Kellogg-Briand Pact and the Nye-Vandenberg resolution for an investigation of the munitions industry were products of their political activity. Throughout the two decades the societies fought military training in schools and colleges.[53]

To pacifists these actions, though worthy, seemed merely to scratch the surface of the problems. They calmed tensions without getting at the primal sources of the tensions. The pacifists, in contrast, boldly set about to probe to the very root of the matter, and in doing so they attracted to their cause a surprising number of liberal and radical thinkers in the fields of education, religion, politics, and labor. Merle Curti, the historian of the American peace movement, has stated that ". . . the increasing vigor and strength of the radical groups was the most promising development in the history of the American struggle against war."[54] Devere Allen writing in the midst of the era said, ". . . we have moved along since the Armistice into a realism the like of which cannot be found in any previous period."[55] A brief sketch of these groups which maintained a pacifist testimony during the inter-war period and the representative individuals who contributed to the literature of the period will provide some estimation of the scope and importance of the movement.

[51] "The Church in Wartime," *The Christian Century,* LVI (December 13, 1939), 1535.

[52] *The New Republic,* XLI (January 14, 1925), 184.

[53] These accomplishments are summarized in Allen, *Fight for Peace,* pp. 47-48; Curti, *Peace or War,* pp. 291-298.

[54] Curti, *Peace or War,* p. 288.

[55] Devere Allen, "The Peace Movement Moves Left," *The Annals* of the American Academy of Political and Social Science, CLXXV (September, 1934), 151.

The "historic peace churches," which have already been discussed at some length, deserve more careful consideration at this point for they provided the seedbed for the nourishment of pacifist ideas. These sects, quietist in origin and, on the whole, feeling themselves out of the mainstream of American life and thought, contributed little to the literature of the period under consideration, yet they continued to provide the only sustained foundation pacifism has ever had in the American experience. In the inter-war period the "sects" were evolving into "churches" as the growing pace of urbanization and industrialization overtook them and begun the tortuous process of molding them into the fabric of American society. The churches, conscious of themselves as "historic peace churches" for the first time, held annual conferences to concert their efforts for peace.[56]

But modernity exacted a toll as well. The impact of social forces in molding these "peculiar" peoples into more standard patterns was nowhere better reflected than in the statistics compiled by Vernon Holloway which showed a significant decline in the number of members of these peace churches who declared themselves as conscientious objectors during the Second World War. By 1945 one-half of Mennonite men eligible for the draft were in regular military service, one-fifth had chosen noncombatant duty, and one-third entered the Civilian Public Service program as conscientious objectors. For every Brethren in Civilian Public Service and in noncombatant duty, there were fifteen in the regular military service. The Quakers were subject to these same trends; three-fourths chose a non-pacifist position.[57] Thus while pacifism was gaining many new adherents as a product of the experience of the First World War, it was losing ground among the very groups that had always given it stability.

The Mennonites, an Anabaptist sect that sprang to life in the turbulence of the Reformation, were organized in Zurich, Switzerland, in 1525 by Menno Simons. Known as the "Bible Students," or "Swiss Brethren," they attracted adherents principally in Switzerland and Holland. Like other Anabaptist groups the Mennonites stressed the literal interpretation of the Scriptures, a life of discipleship, adult baptism, the separation of church and state, freedom of conscience, and nonresistance. Their nonresistance brought them in the centuries following the Reformation endless suffering and persecution. Many Mennonites compromised on nonresistance; those who refused were subject to frequent migrations. From 1788 to 1820 the Mennonites of Germany undertook a mass migration to Russia. In the 1870's and 1880's this trek was repeated as they moved from Russia to the United

[56] Hershberger, *War, Peace, and Nonresistance,* p. 162.

[57] Vernon H. Holloway, "A Review of American Religious Pacifism," *Religion in Life,* XIX (Summer, 1950), 370.

States and Canada. They were not the first of their faith to come to the United States, for a Mennonite congregation was formed in Germantown, Pennsylvania, as early as 1683. By the twentieth century the Mennonites numbered about 100,000 and were primarily an agricultural people attempting to preserve something of their strong tradition of family and church authority. The Mennonites were leaders in campaigning for and establishing the Civilian Public Service camps for conscientious objectors in the Second World War; like the Quakers they have defined their task as peacemakers in terms of bringing relief to the victims of war and disaster.[58]

The Church of the Brethren was organized by Alexander Mach in Western Germany in 1708. Its first American congregation was established in 1723. Until the twentieth century the sect maintained a nonresistance position, but since then it has shown itself amenable like the Quakers to the concepts of the social gospel and to an interest in politics and social life. This has led many of the Brethren to assume a position of nonviolent resistance.[59]

The Society of Friends, founded in England by George Fox in the seventeenth century, has had a remarkable impact in proportion to its numbers upon the religious and political life of Great Britain and the United States. The names of Penn, Benezet, and Woolman are inseparably linked with the formative years of American history. In the beginning, though Fox spoke of a "covenant of peace," the Friends were not absolute nonresistants; the individual conscience was looked upon as determinative. By the nineteenth century the Quakers by means of a maturing concept of the "corporate inner light" (the consensus of the group determined the act of the individual) arrived at a "settled" peace testimony of nonresistance. At the same time the Quakers were moving out of their isolation and quietism and adopting the challenge of remaking the world by working in war and peace to bring relief to the suffering through material aid and good will. The nineteenth century saw an evangelical fire burn brightly among English Quakers such as Wilberforce, Clarkson, Buxton, Gurney, and Bright. The great war on slavery was the result.

In the twentieth century the idea of a "corporate inner light" has broken down and has been replaced to a large extent by a reliance upon the individual conscience once again. Quakers have diverged sharply in terms of liberal and conservative religious thought, often reflective of an urban-rural division. Yet the scope of the Quaker's conception of his responsibility for justice and peace in the world has increased immeasur-

[58] The historical data on the Mennonites are drawn from Hershberger, *War, Peace, and Nonresistance,* pp. 73-86; Sibley and Jacob, *Conscription,* p. 20; Martin, *Pacifism,* pp. 41-45.

[59] The historical data are drawn from Sibley and Jacob, *Conscription,* pp. 20-22.

ably. At the conclusion of the First World War Quakers directed the rebuilding of the Verdun region in France and carried on a program of feeding that reached millions of children. Instrumental in guiding this project was the American Friends Service Committee, one of the finest realizations of the Quaker social conscience. Founded during the First World War, within seven years it was employing six hundred full-time workers and utilizing the services of fifty to sixty thousand assistants in Europe to carry out its work.[60] In all, it distributed food and supplies to six to seven million people in Europe.[61] The Peace Section of this committee led by Ray Newton was one of the most vigorous of the pacifist organizations of the inter-war period; the Peace Association of Friends, with a membership estimated at ninety thousand, provided the solid foundation for the Quaker testimony against war.[62] The Quakers alone among the peace churches were represented in the literature of the pacifist movement in the inter-war period by a distinguished group of scholars who spoke, not so much as Quakers, but as exponents of the liberal religious and political doctrines of the day, for the Quakers showed ". . . the greatest receptivity to the assumptions and arguments of the . . . Protestant social gospel."[63] Most prominent of these spokesmen were Henry Cadbury, Hollis Professor of Divinity at the Divinity School of Harvard University and chairman of the American Friends Service Committee from 1928 to 1934; Rufus Jones, author, interpreter of the Quaker way of life to the American public, and long-time professor of philosophy at Haverford College; D. Elton Trueblood, professor of religion and chaplain of Stanford University from 1936 to 1945; William Hull, John Wharton Professor of History and International Relations at Swarthmore College; and E. Merrill Root, Earlham College literature teacher and poet.[64]

The major Protestant denominations—Methodist, Congregational, Baptist, Lutheran, Presbyterian, Episcopalian, Disciplines of Christ, Evangelical, and Unitarians—have been non-pacifist throughout their history. Both Luther and Calvin taught the doctrine of the "just" war as worked out by Catholic theologians through the centuries of the dominance of the Roman see in Western Europe. But if the most influential preachers and theologians of Protestantism in the inter-war period had had their way, many of these denominations would have repudiated their historic traditions and would have ranged themselves

[60] Charles M. Woodman, *Quakers Find a Way: Their Discoveries in Practical Living* (Indianapolis: The Bobbs-Merrill Company, 1950), p. 242.

[61] *Ibid.*, p. 242.

[62] Ferrell, *Peace in Their Time,* p. 27n.

[63] Vernon H. Holloway, "A Review of American Religious Pacifism," *Religion in Life,* XIX (Summer, 1950), 371.

[64] The historical data on the Quakers are drawn from Jones, *Quakers,* pp. 104-130; Sibley and Jacob, *Conscription,* p. 24; Martin, *Pacifism,* pp. 61-67.

alongside the "peace churches." Through outspoken resolutions, several of these denominational bodies did change camps for at least brief periods of time. Throughout the country the Protestant clergy spoke of the "renunciation," "the excommunication," or the "outlawry" of war. John Knox in 1942 estimated that half the influential Protestant ministers in the country were pacifists;[65] a look at the roster of names would make one wonder if this estimate were not much too low.

Although personal influences and experience no doubt played a significant role in leading these ministers to take their pacifist vows it would seem that the origin of this move was to be found in the social gospel movement. The ministers and theologians who accepted pacifism were those noted for their liberalism. As the elements of their thought are investigated, the impact of the social gospel becomes increasingly apparent. Developed at greater length later in this volume, the path leading from the social gospel to pacifism can be briefly sketched here. The social gospel envisaged the creation of the Kingdom of God on the earth through the efforts of God and man. Maturing in the closing decades of the nineteenth century, it was generally accepted by a sizeable group of ministers and theologians in the major denominations by the First World War. There was no agreed method for achieving the goal; some became Christian Socialists, some adopted a program of social reformism, and still others spoke of various kinds of communal idealism. Most important, however, was the fact that the social gospel thinkers and their disciples failed to consider seriously the problem of war during the years when they were molding and refining their theories.

When Woodrow Wilson pictured the entrance of the United States into the World War as a Great Crusade to exterminate once and for all the evils of war, autocracy, and economic injustice, the social gospel clergy caught a vision of the kingdom arriving in their generation through a "holy war." With rare exceptions they whole-heartedly endorsed the war; many, in fact, served as military chaplains or in Red Cross and Y.M.C.A. work overseas. They soon discovered, to their dismay, that war was far from "holy" and that the peace bore no resemblance at all to the imagined kingdom. In the deep disillusionment of the twenties which they shared with sensitive spirits throughout the land the Protestant clergy, unlike many intellectuals, did not despair of their vision or their ideals but they rejected outright the means they had adopted, and began a search for a method worthy of the goal sought. In keeping with their idealism many saw in pacifism the means they desired. By adding ideals of the social gospel to the developing doctrine of pacifism as held particularly by the Quakers, a union of the

[65] John Knox, "Re-examining Pacifism," *Religion and the Present Crisis.* Edited by John Knox (Chicago: University of Chicago Press, 1942), p. 33.

two was affected that produced the pacifism characteristic of the inter-war period.

Among the prominent Protestant ministers who were pacifists during the period were Ernest Tittle, John Nevin Sayre, Harold Phillips, Kirby Page, Harold Bosley, Edmund Chaffee, Albert Day, Sherwood Eddy, Arthur Swift, Paul Jones, E. Stanley Jones, Harold Fey, Harry Emerson Fosdick, Allan Hunter, Ralph Sockman, Henry Crane, Allan Chalmers, George Buttrick, Bernard Clausen, Paul Scherer, and Bernard Bell.[66] Pacifist theologians and religious educators included George Coe, professor of religious education, Teachers College, Columbia University; S. Ralph Harlow, professor of religion and social ethics, Smith College; Halford Luccock, professor of homiletics, Yale Divinity School; Reinhold Niebuhr, professor of applied Christianity, Union Theological Seminary; Albert Palmer, professor of practical theology and president, Chicago Theological Seminary; Harry Ward, professor of Christian ethics, Union Theological Seminary; John Bennett, professor of Christian theology and philosophy of religion, Pacific School of Religion; H. Richard Niebuhr, professor of Christian ethics, Yale Divinity School; Nels F. S. Ferré, Abbott Professor of Applied Theology, Andover Newton Theological Seminary; Georgia Harkness, professor of applied theology, Garrett Biblical Institute; and Roland Bainton, Titus Street Professor of Ecclesiastical History at the Divinity School of Yale University. This group of scholars and preachers provided pacifism during the period with a stream of literature, books, magazine articles, and pamphlets, that was thoughtful, serious, and challenging.

The patron saint of the Protestant pacifists was John Haynes Holmes. His invigorating personality and far-reaching mind brought him to the leadership of many causes dear to the hearts of liberals. Born in Philadelphia, November 29, 1879, Holmes grew up and received his education in Boston. He finished his work at Harvard University in three years, graduating *summa cum laude* in 1902, with his major studies in philosophy and history. Entering Harvard Divinity School he received his Bachelor of Sacred Theology degree in 1904, was ordained into the ministry of the Unitarian Church, and was installed as pastor of the church at Dorchester, Massachusetts. It was in New York, however, that Holmes was to find his field of service for the rest of his life. In 1907 he acepted a call to the wealthy, conservative Church of the Messiah in New York. Not content with a position of high leadership in the Unitarian church, Holmes put his searching mind to work and soon found himself both a Socialist and a pacifist. Within

[66] Biographical data on those men who made significant contributions to the pacifist literature of the period will be found in the biographical guides listed in the bibliography.

his church the principle of freedom of thought was established as the guiding spirit for worship and fellowship.

Holmes was one of the very few pacifists who remained faithful to his vows during the First World War. It was, perhaps, this act of courage more than any other deed in his life that gained for him the respect accorded during the following decades. A serious question may be raised about how aptly the term "Protestant" applied to the thought and actions of Holmes, for they were sometimes extravagant and always ultra-liberal. In 1919, he resigned from the Unitarian ministry, his church became independent and nondenominational and changed its name to the Community Church, opening its doors to Jews, Catholics, Hindus, in fact, to anyone who wished to join. The church was unified not by any theological belief, but by a "democratic social idealism." This spirit was reflected in the endless activities in which Holmes participated; he was the moving spirit in such varied organizations as the National Association for the Advancement of the Colored People, American Civil Liberties Union, All World Gandhi Fellowship, War Resisters' League, and the City Affairs Commission of New York City.

Holmes edited *Unity,* the periodical in which the first complete plans for the outlawry of war movement were published. An inveterate "theatregoer," he penned a play together with Reginald Lawrence entitled "If This Be Treason" that was produced by the Theatre Guild in New York in 1935. The play portrayed the potential power of pacifism in political affairs. The books he wrote on the relation of religion to social problems had a deep influence on pacifist thought.

The importance of John Haynes Holmes to the study of the pacifist movement in the inter-war period rests in the vivid illustration he affords of the matrix of ideas and causes of which pacifism was only a segment. Pacifism was an element of the intense desire of men of the character of Holmes to breathe into all the social relationships of life the spiritual values of love, good will, and trust.[67]

Pacifism was more than the toy of a few guiding lights on the Protestant horizon; it permeated into the rank and file of clergymen as well. In 1931, and again in 1934, the periodical *The World Tomorrow,* under the guidance of its editor Kirby Page, conducted a poll among the Protestant clergy on problems of peace and war. In 1931, questionnaires were mailed to 53,000 ministers, about half the Protestant clergy in the United States. Out of 19,372 who replied to the poll, 10,427 ministers (54 per cent) stated that it was their ". . . present purpose not to sanction any future war or participate as an armed combatant." A larger

[67] The biographical data on Holmes are found in "Preacher Without Authority: The Story of John Haynes Holmes," *The World Tomorrow,* XIII (March, 1930), 119-122; *Who's Who in America: A Biographical Dictionary of Notable Living Men and Women* (Chicago: A. N. Marquis Company, 1954), XXVIII, 1261.

number, 12,076 (62 per cent), desired the church to state that it would refuse to support or sanction another war. Whatever the methodological limitations, the poll did reveal the deep inroads pacifism had made in Protestantism.[68] A surprised *Christian Century* saw in it an, ". . . almost unbelievable courage. . . . A distinct counter-tendency to extricate religion from all these conformities and compromises and to establish its own moral sovereignty."[69]

In the 1934 poll, 100,490 questionnaires were sent to ministers of all the major denominations and to Jewish rabbis. The questionnaire, including this time a set of questions dealing with problems of economic justice, received a much lower percentage of replies: 20,870 (21 per cent). Again a remarkable number of respondents, 12,904 (62 per cent), indicated they were willing to refuse as individuals to support and sanction war; 13,997 (67 per cent) called on the churches to take a similar stand. Larger numbers than these voted for a substantial reduction of armaments, and the abandoning of the policy of armed intervention in other lands to protect the property or personal rights of American citizens. By church groups, the Methodists, the Disciples, and the Congregationalists ranked consistently at the top of the pacifist column.[70] It is interesting to note that these same three churches were also the ones in American Protestantism most permeated by the social gospel.

The churches took their stand against war as well. Devere Allen felt that ". . . nothing more fantastic could have been imagined . . . than the rush of clergymen and huge denominational bodies of Christians and Jews to embrace, in official resolutions and in specific day-by-day religious and educational programs . . . the renunciation of war."[71] Walter W. Van Kirk's *Religion Renounces War* described and analyzed this rash of resolutions against war that swept through the Protestant denominations in the inter-war period.[72] Paul Hutchinson, in the same year, stated that twenty million members of Protestant churches had been pledged by their official church bodies to oppose all war.[73] The crucial question was: how many people

[68] Kirby Page, "Nineteen Thousand Clergymen on War and Peace," *The World Tomorrow,* XIV (May, 1931), 138-154.

[69] "Ministers and War," *The Christian Century,* XLVIII (May 6, 1931), 598, 599.

[70] Kirby Page, "20,870 Clergymen on War and Economic Injustice," *The World Tomorrow,* XVII (May 10, 1934), 222-256.

[71] Devere Allen, "The Peace Movement Moves Left," *The Annals* of the American Academy of Political and Social Science, CLXXV (September, 1934), 154.

[72] Walter W. Van Kirk, *Religion Renounces War* (Chicago: Willett, Clark and Company, 1934).

[73] Paul Hutchinson, "The Collapse of Pacifism," *Scribner's Magazine,* XCV (June, 1934), 399.

in the pews were aware of these actions? On the whole it is probably fair to judge that the pulpit was far more pacifist than the pew, though a peace poll taken by the Congregational Council for Social Action of 200,000 members indicated that pacifist ideas had had some visible effect on Congregational laymen. Fifteen per cent indicated that they had arrived at a position of absolute pacifism.[74] It was these strong elements of the Protestant clergy and churches committed to the social gospel that provided the dynamics of leadership, thought, and action for the pacifism of the inter-war period.[75]

The traditional Catholic doctrine of the "just" war worked out by theologians such as Augustine and Thomas Aquinas, and the centralized authority of the church meant that there were few Catholics in the pacifist ranks. Charles Plater observed that ". . . war cannot be unchristian because, if it were, the Church would have grievously and permanently erred in a capital point of morality."[76] No Catholic cared to challenge the Church's authority to pronounce judgment on the justice of each war, or her authority as the interpreter of the Gospels.

Nevertheless a few Catholics did accept pacifism. A few, especially those in the Catholic Worker group in the United States, based their stand on the theological qualifications for a "just" war. No modern war could possibly satisfy such requirements as: (a) the war must spare non-combatants; (b) the war must be defensive; (c) the war must be waged with civilized weapons; or (d) one side must be clearly in the right.[77] Therefore pacifism was the only possible position because no modern war could be a "just" war. These pacifists found consolation in the fact that the Pope had never prohibited absolute pacifism. A second group of Catholics came to a pacifist position for reasons of short term political expediency; they were adherents of the isolationism

[74] *The Christian Century,* LIII (January 22, 1936), 132.

[75] Some observers were not as enthusiastic about this trend in Protestantism. J. E. O'Sullivan writing in the *National Republic* said: "It therefore begins to appear that the enemy that has been actively sowing the seed of revolt and engineering its pernicious program to wreck the American Constitution and its institutions, the church and the home and to win over the youth of the land is now beginning to reap its harvest and this in the name of 'modernism' and 'humanism'." J. E. O'Sullivan, "Some Ministers in Revolt," *National Republic,* XXII (June, 1934), 29; General Douglas MacArthur commented: "Should not these clergymen turn their attention to the individual sinner and rid the country of crime rather than attack the national keepers of peace. . . . History teaches us that religion and patriotism have always gone hand in hand, while atheism has invariably been accompanied by radicalism, communism, bolshevism, and other enemies of free government." Douglas MacArthur to the Editors of *The World Tomorrow, The World Tomorrow,* XIV (June, 1931), 192, 193.

[76] Charles Plater, *A Primer of Peace and War: The Principles of International Morality* (New York: P. J. Kennedy and Sons, 1915), p. 113.

[77] Herman Hoffmann, "Pacifism and the Catholic Church," *The World Tomorrow,* XV (April, 1932), 118.

of Father Coughlin.[78] A third group, and one representative of an ancient tradition in Catholic life, claimed the doctrine of vocation as their justification for a position of pacifism.[79] The Church has always revered those individuals who have felt called to live otherworldly lives in strict obedience to the counsels of the Scriptures. The Church has held that scriptural counsels of perfection could never be considered as commands for the state, for its task is a worldly one of protecting its subjects, but for the individual such a path was worthy of the highest honor.

Most prominent among the Catholic pacifists was the poet, Benjamin Francis Musser. A converted Episcopalian, Musser entered the Third Order of St. Francis in 1909. In 1934 he was appointed the first Poet Laureate of New Jersey. His pacifism was an intense expression of his obedience to the scriptural counsels of perfection.[80]

For most American Catholics, however, the traditional doctrine of the Church that man has an inherent natural right of self-preservation defined their position on the problem of war. *The Commonweal* told its readers that ". . . the Church agrees with the common sense of mankind in holding that war is not always evil, and that a just war—such as one of defense against aggression—must be supported as a strict duty of citizenship."[81] There was not a little irony in the fact that the Catholic Church was upholding the "strict duty of citizenship" against a large segment of American Protestantism which was advocating the refusal to participate in any further call to arms by the nation. The myth of American nativists received a curious twist.

A few Jewish rabbis enthusiastically supported the Protestant drive against war. One prominent man of letters, Ludwig Lewisohn, conceived of pacifism as an integral part of Jewish ethical humanism. With the rise of Hitler and his pogroms, however, there were few Jews who felt a disposition to embrace pacifism.

There were, in addition, a number of small religious sects which refused to support war for a variety of reasons. In the Atlanta Penitentiary during the First World War, as a political prisoner along with Eugene Debs, was the religious extremist, J. F. Rutherford. Released from prison in 1919, Rutherford assumed the leadership of the Jehovah's Witnesses, the most bizarre element in the pacifist ranks. One could hardly imagine a greater contrast than that between the social gospel liberals and this band of apocalyptic fundamentalists. The Witnesses,

[78] Vernon H. Holloway, "A Review of American Religious Pacifism," *Religion in Life,* XIX (Summer, 1950), 376.

[79] Sibley and Jacob, *Conscription,* p. 29.

[80] *Catholic Authors: Contemporary Biographical Sketches 1930-1947.* Edited by Matthew Hoehn (Newark: St. Mary's Abbey, 1948), pp. 566-567.

[81] The Problem of Pacifism," *The Commonweal,* XIII (April 29, 1931), 702; Martin, *Pacifism,* pp. 26-45.

founded in 1874 by Reverend Charles Taze Russell, a Congregational minister, believed that all earthly governments were a part of the devil's empire. They foresaw that soon a union of the democratic and totalitarian governments would occur at which time the great battle of Armageddon would take place, when the "Theocracy of the Lord" would crush the kingdoms of this world. The pacifism of the Jehovah's Witnesses stemmed from their refusal to give any allegiance to any earthly government. The rapid growth of this sect provided, and continues to provide, an important segment of the pacifist movement, though their objection to war has no relation to an objection to physical violence.[82]

The Christodelphians, another premillenialist sect, were nonresistants on the basis of fulfilling the counsels of the Sermon on the Mount; they have gone to the extent of disowning members who entered the military service.[83] The Seventh Day Adventists adopted a noncombatant position. They were willing to participate in the war effort as long as they did not have to take a direct part in killing.[84] Other groups which refused to support the Second World War were the Negro Moslems, Mankind United, a California religious group, and the Hopi Indian religionists who were nonresistants.[85]

The road to pacifism was not always through the church. Individuals through their liberal or radical political philosophies have arrived by themselves at such a position. No generalizations can be hazarded about these men; each made the way in his own distinctive manner. Radical thinkers like Roger Baldwin, director of the American Civil Liberties Union, imprisoned during the First World War as a conscientious objector, and Scott Nearing, sociologist, economist, free lance writer, member of the Communist Party from 1926 to 1929, were both philosophical anarchists.[86] Albert Guerard, professor of general literature at Stanford University, Otto Glaser, professor of biology at Amherst, and Robert Herrick, author and long-time professor of English at the University of Chicago were among the distinguished liberals in the pacifist ranks.

The trait noted in the life and activities of John Haynes Holmes of the interweaving of pacifism into a pattern of liberal reformism was evident, as well, in the most influential of these philosophical pacifists:

[82] J. G. St. Clair Drake, "Who Are Jehovah's Witnesses?" *The Christian Century,* LIII (April 15, 1936), 567-570; Sibley and Jacob, *Conscription,* pp. 31-35; Martin, *Pacifism,* pp. 188-189.

[83] Sibley and Jacob, *Conscription,* p. 36; Martin, *Pacifism,* pp. 188-189.

[84] Vernon H. Holloway, "A Review of American Religious Pacifism," *Religion in Life,* XIX (Summer, 1950), 376.

[85] Sibley and Jacob, *Conscription,* p. 36.

[86] "Galahad of Freedom: The Story of Roger Baldwin," *The World Tomorrow,* XIII (January, 1930), 33-36; "A Puritan Revolutionist: The Story of Scott Nearing," *The World Tomorrow,* XIII (July, 1930), 305-308.

Oswald Garrison Villard. Villard traced the origins of his pacifism to revulsion at the Spanish American War. The preparation for such a stand, however, had really begun earlier, for his mother was the only daughter of William Lloyd Garrison, and his father, Henry Villard, the railroad financier, had arrived at a pacifist position while a war correspondent during the Civil War. Never were pacifist ideas presented to a more distinguished audience of the nation's intellectual aristocracy than by Villard through the pages of the New York *Evening Post,* owned and edited by him from 1897-1918, and *The Nation,* which he owned and edited from 1918-1932, and for which he continued as contributing editor until 1940. Villard's liberal credo was best expressed by himself: "To be opposed to war; to hold no hate for any peoples; to be determined to champion a better world, to believe in the equality of all men and women; and to be opposed to all tyrants and all suppression of liberty and conscience and beliefs. . . ."[87]

Villard's fighting instinct—he developed a strong interest in military strategy and tactics—was expended on behalf of causes as varied as women's suffrage, Negro education in the South, Negro equality (as a founder of the National Association for the Advancement of the Colored People), the emancipation of labor, and the extermination of the Tammany political machine. The political philosophy at the core of Villard's pacifism was revealed in the shock he felt when Congress voted the Declaration of War in April, 1917: "It came nearer to unmanning me than anything in my life. For I knew, as I knew that I lived, that this ended the republic as we had known it; that henceforth we Americans were to be part and parcel of world politics, rivalries, jealousies, and militarism; that hate, prejudice, and passion were now enthroned in the United States. . . . The fundamental foreign policy of the republic—to remain aloof from the jealousies, intrigues, and wars of Europe—was thus overthrown."[88]

More than once the pacifist movement was dismissed by contemporaries as a ". . . subdivision of the women's club phenomenon;"[89] American clubwomen of the twenties and thirties were said to spend their leisure hours ". . . tatting doilies of peace. . . ."[90] There is in the

[87] Oswald Garrison Villard, *Fighting Years: Memoirs of a Liberal Editor* (New York: Harcourt, Brace and Company, 1939), p. 376. (Hereinafter cited as Villard, *Fighting Years.*)

[88] *Ibid.*, pp. 324, 326; Biographical material on Villard is from Villard, *Fighting Years, passim;* "Trumpet to the People: The Story of Oswald Garrison Villard," *The World Tomorrow,* XIII (November, 1930), 440-443.

[89] Bruce Bliven, "They Cry 'Peace, Peace.' III. Neutrality Is Not Enough," *The New Republic,* LXXXV (November 20, 1935), 39.

[90] Henry Morton Robinson, *Fantastic Interim: A Hindsight History of American Manners, Morals, and Mistakes Between Versailles and Pearl Harbor* (New York: Harcourt, Brace and Company, 1943), p. 191.

American folklore, if not in the common traditions of mankind from the beginning, the notion that women and peace are almost synonymous terms; that if only women were admitted to the councils of state war would be no more. American women have not been disposed to challenge the idea, but have made enthusiastic attempts by banding together in large organizations to wage the war on war. Devere Allen, recalling by way of contrast, the innumerable instances of women zealously supporting at home, or even on the battlefields, their soldier husbands or sons, commented, ". . . seekers for a vital difference of behavior between the male and female sexes would need more than a powerful microscope; he [sic] would require the lenses of imagination."[91] Yet he also succumbed to the myth declaring ". . . they are . . . an oasis in a desert of apathy, fairweather pacifism, and male-minded conformity."[92] In the inter-war period women pacifists in the tradition of Julia Ward Howe, Lucretia Mott, and Belva Lockwood formed a significant part of the pacifist movement.

At The Hague in 1915, the Women's International Committee for Permanent Peace with Jane Addams, the foremost American woman pacifist, as chairman, proposed the idea of a conference of neutral nations that would offer continuous mediation between the belligerent forces in Europe. Though this suggestion had no practical consequence in regard to the war, the experience of women meeting together from many nations was fruitful; the committee evolved into the Women's International League for Peace and Freedom, the American section of which, with its headquarters in Washington, was one of the two or three most important pacifist organizations in the United States.[93] Jane Addams, founder of Chicago's Hull House and recipient of the Nobel Peace Prize for 1931, continued as chairman of the Women's International League, directing its rapid growth, until by 1927 it had over fifty thousand members in twenty-five countries.[94] The American section, with a membership exceeding twelve thousand, was the one women's peace group organized into state and local chapters.[95] The League's most notable activity was the political lobbying carried on in Washington under the direction of Dorothy Detzer, who was given personal credit for inspiring the Nye munitions investigation of 1935.[96]

Two similar pacifist societies, smaller in scope and more limited in their activities, were the Women's Peace Union of the Western Hemisphere, and the Women's Peace Society, founded by Fanny Garrison

[91] Allen, *Fight for Peace,* p. 284.
[92] *Ibid.,* p. 289.
[93] Curti, *Peace or War,* p. 272.
[94] Allen, *Fight for Peace,* p. 287.
[95] John W. Masland, "Pressure Groups and American Foreign Policy," *The Public Opinion Quarterly,* VI (Spring, 1942), 115.
[96] *Ibid.,* 115.

Villard in 1919. The pledge of the Women's Peace Union illustrates the acceptance of radical pacifism by these women's groups: "I affirm it is my intention never to aid in or sanction war, offensive or defensive, international or civil, in any way, whether by making or handling munitions, subscribing to war loans, using my labor for the purpose of setting others free for war service, helping by money or work any relief organization which supports or condones war."[97] The giant among the women's peace societies, the National Committee on the Cause and Cure of War, with its eleven affiliated women's organizations representing nearly six million American women, was a conservative group interested in arbitration, disarmament, the World Court, and the Kellogg-Briand Pact, but it never adopted the pacifist stand against war.[98]

The noisiest of the pacifists were the college students. It is impossible to tell to what extent their protest was an expression of genuine pacifism, a popular rejection of war in the spirit of disillusionment, or an attractive issue by which a new generation could assert its independence. At least, the student demonstrations for peace caught the public eye. A student strike, for example, held simultaneously on college and university campuses throughout the United States April 2, 1936, brought an estimated 500,000 to 750,000 students out of the classrooms to parade for peace.[99] At Harvard, a "Committee for the Recognition of Classroom Generals" was engaged in distributing toy medals to interventionist-minded professors.[100] Students wearing gas masks picketed the classroom of one such professor.[101]

Pacifist sentiment among college students after the First World War seems to have first manifested itself at the Student Volunteer Convention in Indianapolis, in 1923, when a group of students pledged to refuse to participate in any war; it was ". . . the first articulate expression of American youth in revolt against the traditional position of accepting war as a necessary evil."[102] Similar expressions occurred at the Evanston meeting of the Interdenominational Student Conference in 1925,[103] at the Northwestern University campus the same year, where the presence of thirty-eight pacifist converts aroused the campus community to the extent of holding mass meetings to bring the wandering ones back to sanity,[104] and at the Milwaukee Conference of the Council

[97] *The World Tomorrow,* V (December, 1922), 375.
[98] Allen, *Fight for Peace,* p. 287.
[99] "Students and War," *The Christian Century,* LII (May 6, 1936), 656.
[100] Irwin Ross, "College Students and the War," *The New Republic,* CIII (July 15, 1940), 80.
[101] *Ibid.,* 80.
[102] *The World Tomorrow,* VII (February, 1924), 57.
[103] *The World Tomorrow,* IX (February, 1926), 57.
[104] C. DeWitt Norton, "Will History Repeat Itself?" *The Survey,* LIII (February 15, 1925), 593-595.

of Christian Associations in 1927.[105] Harold Seidman estimated in 1933 that twenty-three thousand college students had taken the pacifist pledge.[106] The most famous poll, conducted by the Brown University *Daily Herald,* the Intercollegiate Disarmament Council, and the National Student Federation of America in 1933, and inspired by the dramatic evidences of pacifism in British universities, reflected the views of 21,725 students in 65 colleges and universities. A position of uncompromising pacifism was taken by 8,415 students (39 percent).[107]

A strong peace sentiment was evident in the radical youth movements. The United Youth Conference Against War, meeting in New York in 1932, denounced capitalism as the breeder of war.[108] In 1934, Socialist and Communist directed youth groups formed the American Youth Congress, which through its affiliated members represented over a million young people. The Congress resolved to wage a war on the R.O.T.C.; from the impact of this group came the first student strike against war.[109] The experience of the American Youth Congress led in 1935 to the organization of the American Student Union, which joined with Christian youth groups to set up the United Student Peace Committee and to adopt a platform calling for a constitutional amendment to end compulsory military training in colleges and universities, the maintenance of civil rights, and the support of those who had taken the Oxford pledge.[110] In 1938, another committee, the Youth Committee Against War, was formed by youth representatives of the War Resisters' League, the Fellowship of Reconciliation, the American Friends Service Committee, the National Council of Methodist Youth, and the Young People's Socialist League.[111]

The most dramatic expression of college feeling, in terms of propaganda value at least, was the Veterans of Future Wars, which grew out of a practical joke among a group of upperclassmen in a Princeton University eating club, and which spread rapidly to include three hundred chapters on American college campuses. The program of the Veterans—". . . a $1,000 bonus for each prospective fighter, due June 1,

[105] Kirby Page, "When College Students Get Together," *The World Tomorrow,* X (February, 1927), 76-77.

[106] Harold Seidman, "How Radical Are College Students?" *The American Scholar,* IV (Summer, 1935), 326.

[107] Harold Seidman, "The Colleges Renounce War," *The Nation,* CXXXVI (May 17, 1933), 554-555; *The World Tomorrow,* XVI (April 12, 1933), 341; *The World Tomorrow,* XVI (June, 1933), 415; *The Nation,* CXXXVI (May 24, 1933), 571.

[108] *The World Tomorrow,* XV (December 7, 1932), 531-532.

[109] Thomas F. Neblett, "Youth Movements in the United States," *The Annals of the American Academy of Political and Social Science,* CXCIV (November, 1937), 146-147.

[110] *Ibid.,* 147.

[111] *The New Republic,* CIV (January 27, 1941), 112.

1965 but to be paid now with retroactive three per cent interest compounded semi-annually for thirty years back to June 1, 1935 . . ."[112]—was a telling attack on the ambitions and tactics of the American Legion and the Veterans of Foreign Wars. It was an idea with imaginative appeal to all elements of the college population, a quality rarely discovered in the pacifist peace program.

The impression must be avoided, however, that more than a small minority of college students were actively concerned with the problems of peace, and a still smaller group advocates of pacifism. Yet the presence of an active concern on the part of this campus minority aroused a strong debate as to its significance. Critics saw in the movement the moral flabbiness of modern youth, the fruit of the decline of classical education, a pragmatic, drifting cynicism toward the issues of life. Certainly much of this student sentiment was isolationist, rather than pacifist; "As a result of two decades of faithful tutelage by their formerly disillusioned elders, students profess to understand both the causes and effects of wars and are determined to keep out of them. . . . The suspicion of Roosevelt, of Congress, of the entire older generation—lies at the heart of youth's attitude toward the war."[113] Bernard DeVoto and Paul Cram considered it a reflection of economic insecurity and the uncertain employment future for students matriculating during, and after, the depression.[114] The liberal journals, in contrast, saw in the movement the awakening of American youth to the realities of national economic and political life. *The Christian Century* commented: "To find among such students this complete disillusionment with respect to war, and the patriotism of former soldiers, is the best protection against future resort to arms."[115] *The Nation* seconded this by noting: "In the chaotic and instructive years since 1918 the emphasis has shifted to the futility and stupidity of war—concrete arguments which carry more force than moral abstractions to a generation raised in disillusionment."[116] Bruce Bliven, editor of *The New Republic,* believed that college students had ". . . gone far beyond the shallow emotionalism of conscientious objection to an understanding of the forces that make for war . . ."[117]

Robert Ferrell, the historian of the "Outlawry of War" movement that led to the Kellogg-Briand Pact, has said of the pacifist organiza-

[112] "Students and War," *The Christian Century,* LIII (May 6, 1936), 656.

[113] Irwin Ross, "College Students and the War," *The New Republic,* CIII (July 15, 1940), 79, 80.

[114] Bernard DeVoto, "Either—Or," *Harpers Monthly Magazine,* CLXXXIII (August, 1941), 333-336; Paul P. Cram, "Undergraduates and the War," *The Atlantic Monthly,* CLXVI (October, 1940), 410-421.

[115] "Students and War," *The Christian Century,* LIII (May 6, 1936), 657.

[116] *The Nation,* CXXXVI (April 12, 1933), 387.

[117] Bruce Bliven, "They Cry 'Peace, Peace.' III. Neutrality Is Not Enough," *The New Republic,* LXXXV (November 20, 1935), 39.

tions: "They were the evangelists of the peace movement. Like Paul on the road to Damascus each had seen a sign and heard a call."[118] The specifically pacifist organizations were small, severely handicapped by a lack of funds, but, nevertheless, quite effective. The National Council for Prevention of War was the largest of these groups. It served as a clearing house in Washington for seventeen pacifist groups, directing propaganda and lobbying activities for the whole movement. Called by one observer ". . . the most effective peace agency in America. . . ."[119]—a remarkable tribute considering the competition from the Carnegie Endowment and the World Peace Foundation with their heavy income and extensive staffs—, the National Council owed whatever it achieved to its executive secretary, Frederick J. Libby, a pacifist Friend. Working with an annual budget of $150,000 and a staff of eighty, Libby conducted a full scale propaganda effort, using the latest devices known to public opinion experts, including a lobbying campaign for pacifist measures employing the services of Jeanette Rankin, ". . . shrewd, well-informed, and brilliant tactician."[120] The National Council, in the opinion of Ferrell, ". . . during the twenties laid down a barrage of peace propaganda the like of which has seldom been seen in the United States."[121]

The Fellowship of Reconciliation, best known of the religious pacifist organizations, was formed in the United States in 1915, under the guidance of Henry Hodgkin, an English Quaker who was instrumental in the founding of the English Fellowship of Reconciliation a year before. Until the mid-thirties, the American Fellowship was the largest organized body of war resisters in the world, including in its membership such notables as Norman Thomas, Reinhold Niebuhr, John Nevin Sayre, Kirby Page, and John Haynes Holmes.[122] The group had a remarkable growth from 68 in 1915 to 13,800 in 1942.[123] The Fellowship program reflected broader interests than pacifism; practical service activities such as the mission to Nicaragua in conjunction with the Quakers during the American intervention in 1927, racial relations, treatment of social offenders, and the desire to work for a just social and economic order were among the projects of the society.[124] A Union Theological

[118] Ferrell, *Peace in Their Time,* p. 26.

[119] Herbert Wilton Stanley, "Red Fascism," *The American Mercury,* XXXVIII (August, 1936), 403.

[120] Curti, *Peace or War,* pp. 276, 273, 277; Herbert Wilton Stanley, "Red Fascism," *The American Mercury,* XXXVIII (August, 1936), 403-404.

[121] Ferrell, *Peace in Their Time,* p. 28.

[122] Devere Allen, "The Peace Movement Moves Left," *The Annals* of the American Academy of Political and Social Science, CLXXV (September, 1934), 153.

[123] Vernon H. Holloway, "A Review of American Religious Pacifism," *Religion in Life,* XIX (Summer, 1950), 374.

[124] *The World Tomorrow,* XIV (May, 1931), 137.

Seminary student did a revealing analysis of the Fellowship's membership in 1929 that tells a great deal, not only about this one group, but of the makeup of the liberal pacifist movement of the whole period. He found that the vast majority of the membership was between the ages twenty to forty. Most interesting was the exceptionally high educational level. Of the total membership, 50 percent had done graduate work, 67 percent were graduates of colleges, 84 percent had studied in college, and 88 percent had finished high school. The percentage of the native-born was higher than that of the general population. Political affiliations were generally middle-of-the-road; only 11 percent had voted either for progressive or radical tickets in the 1928 election—a percentage lower than that of the general population. As to religious interests, 88.5 percent belonged to a church; 75 percent attended regularly; and the predominant denominational ties were Methodist, Society of Friends, Congregational, Presbyterian, and Episcopalian. The three newspapers most widely read were the New York *Times,* the New York *World,* and the Chicago *Tribune*; the three magazines most popular with the group were *The World Tomorrow, The Christian Century,* and *The Nation.*[125] The Fellowship of Reconciliation functioned as the intellectual nerve-center of the pacifist movement; members of this group were responsible for almost the entire pacifist literature of the inter-war period.

Other societies of lesser import and more limited purpose included the Committee on Militarism in Education, a propaganda organization formed to fight the military training program in colleges and high schools, and the War Resisters' League, an affiliate of the War Resisters' International which had as its purpose the banding together of conscientious objectors to secure recognition by governments of their political right to exercise conscientious objection, and to aid those who were imprisoned or persecuted for their pacifist stand. In addition there were the American Committee for the Outlawry of War, American Goodwill Association, Arbitration Crusade, Fellowship for a Christian Social Order, Intercollegiate Peace Association, Catholic Association for

[125] Don M. Chase, "What Sort of People are Pacifists?" *The World Tomorrow,* XII (February, 1929), 83-84. A psychological study done through a questionnaire given to one thousand University of Chicago students in 1928, provides further information on the makeup of the pacifist. The researcher concluded that education is influential in modifying attitudes toward pacifism; men tend to be slightly more militaristic than women; there is no correlation between pacifism and intelligence or neurotic scores; students in the exact sciences tend to be less pacifistic than those in social sciences, languages, or literature; Socialists are more pacifistic than Republicans or Democrats; Catholics and Lutherans are most militaristic of ten churches examined; war service seems to influence men in the militaristic direction rather than pacifistic; and students of mixed and foreign parentage tend to be more pacifistic than the native-born. D. D. Droba, "Effect of Various Factors on Militarism-Pacifism," *The Journal of Abnormal and Social Psychology,* XXVI (July-September, 1931), 141-153.

International Peace, Corda Fratres Association of Cosmopolitan Clubs, Parliament of Peace and Universal Brotherhood, Peace Heroes Memorial Society, School World Friendship League, Society to Eliminate Economic Causes of War, World Peace Association, and the World Peace Mission.[126]

One fond dream beguiled pacifists throughout the interwar period. If the laboring classes of all nations could band together on the basis of their common interests and agree to refuse to support any government which took steps leading to war, peace would become a reality. This had been the vision of the European Socialists prior to the First World War—a vision that quickly evaporated in 1914 as labor rallied to the support of its respective governments. But the vision was revived, and there seemed for awhile, at least, a chance that the widespread belief in the futility of war would make possible its realization. From Europe in the twenties came hopeful reports of the actions of important, representative bodies of labor. Such groups as the International Textile Workers, the International Miners Congress, the International Trades Union Congress, and the British Independent Labour Party endorsed anti-war resolutions.[127] The International Federation of Trade Unions, meeting in Amsterdam in 1922, and supposedly speaking for twenty-five million workers, called for a general international strike in the event of the outbreak of war.[128]

To the despair of pacifists, Socialists, and radical leaders, the forces of labor in the United States were far from being ready or willing to take such a stand. The American Federation of Labor was piously conservative. It had faithfully supported the Spanish American War and the First World War. In 1920, it withdrew from its international ties and joined a regional group, the Pan-American Federation of Labor, partly, no doubt, because of its violent antipathy to Russia.[129] Its Committee on International Labor Relations, in 1927, emphatically announced that labor was not pacifist, and that it intended to fight for honor, justice, freedom, and self-preservation.[130] The A. F. of L. peace program included arbitration, disarmament, government ownership of the munitions industry, and support of the League of Nations, the World Court, and the Kellogg-Briand Pact, but not pacifism.[131]

[126] These organizations are listed by Ferrell, *Peace in Their Time,* pp. 27n-28n.

[127] Devere Allen, "War Resistance Old and New," *The World Tomorrow,* XIV (November, 1931), 364.

[128] A. J. Muste, "Labor's Fight Against War," *The World Tomorrow,* V (November, 1922), 340-342.

[129] William P. Maddox, "Is American Labor Pacifist?" *The American Scholar,* IV (Winter, 1935), 95.

[130] *Ibid.,* 93.

[131] *Ibid.,* 91.

The only ray of light came from the weak Socialist Party, led by Norman Thomas, a courageous pacifist. At the Detroit convention of the party in June, 1934, warning that they would cooperate in a general international strike in the event of war, the Socialists declared, "War cannot be tolerated by Socialists, or preparedness for war. They will unitedly seek to develop trustworthy working class instruments for the peaceable settlement of international disputes and conflicts. . . ."[132]

By the mid-thirties, even the once bright European picture had dimmed considerably. A. J. Muste, leader of the Trotskyite wing of the revolutionary socialist labor movement in the early thirties, returned from a European trip in 1936 with a somber view of the European labor scene: "Inextricably mingled with and in the end corrupting, thwarting, largely defeating all that is fine, idealistic, courageous, self-sacrificing in the proletarian movement is the philosophy of power, the will to power, the desire to humiliate and dominate over or destroy the opponent, the acceptance of the methods of violence and deceit, the theory that the 'end justifies the means.' "[133] The socialist party in power in France in 1936 was arming at a faster rate than its predecessors; Russia was fast becoming an armed bastion; and, by 1938, a three-way split had developed in the British labor movement on the question of war and peace. The labor forces in the United States and abroad were a source of deep disappointment to the pacifist movement.

Though labor proved to be a disappointment, other encouraging developments abroad inspired the pacifist movement in the United States. The most dramatic episode of the two decades took place on February 9, 1933, in the rooms of the debating society of Oxford University. The Oxford Union voted 275-153 that: "This House will, under no circumstances fight for its king and country." The vote was reaffirmed on March 2, 1933, by the overwhelming margin of 750-138.[134] The "Oxford Pledge" held firm until 1938, when, by a 99-58 vote, the Union went on record in support of an ". . . alliance of peaceful nations. . . ."[135] The Oxford revolt was not the beginning, but only a symptom of feelings that had been mounting since the Armistice. No nation in the world had a pacifist movement with as wide a base of public support as did Great Britain.

An event less well publicized, but of wider significance, was the

[132] Devere Allen, "The Peace Movement Moves Left," *The Annals* of the American Academy of Political and Social Science, CLXXV (September, 1934), 155.

[133] A. J. Muste, "Return to Pacifism," *The Christian Century*, LIII (December 2, 1936), 1604.

[134] *The Nation*, CXXXVI (March 15, 1933), 275.

[135] Allan Armstrong Hunter, "Will England's Pacifists Stick?" *The Christian Century*, LV (September 28, 1938), 1154.

Ponsonby Peace Letter of 1927. Sir Arthur Ponsonby, an ex-Under-Secretary of State for Foreign Affairs, obtained the signatures of 128,770 persons, within a few months time, to a letter which included the statement: ". . . we shall refuse to support or render war service to any Government which resorts to arms. . . ."[136] One year after the Oxford vote, which was seconded by many British universities, a letter appeared in the British press, signed by Canon H. R. L. Sheppard, one of England's popular preachers, asking those who had resolved to renounce war to send him a postcard. The response was amazing; in twelve months he had received 80,000 names; by 1937, there were 130,000.[137] This response resulted in the formation of the Peace Pledge Union.

England was not alone in having a pacifist movement. Though in most European nations the groups were small, they did reach sizable proportions in Germany and France. Several organizations maintained an international program. The War Resisters' International grew rapidly from 985 members in 21 countries in 1928, to over 9,000 members in 24 countries a decade later.[138] The International Fellowship of Reconciliation extended its program to twenty-six nations during the period.[139] In 1928, an International Union of Anti-Militarist Clergymen met for the first time in Amsterdam, Holland.[140] A more mysterious association was the "Army of Men Without Hate," comprising war resisters from fourteen nations of Europe, led by Colonel Ernst Ceresole of Switzerland, which would appear on occasions of natural disaster, as an avalanche in Switzerland or a flood in Liechtenstein, and volunteer its services in reconstructing the area.[141]

Perhaps the knowledge that important intellectual leaders and men of affairs throughout the world had accepted pacifism was of even greater encouragement. In England, especially, the pacifist ranks were filled with famous individuals. Aldous Huxley, Virginia Woolf, Clive Bell, Roger Fry, Laurence Housman, Sir Arthur Ponsonby, Bertrand Russell, Siegfried Sassoon, Sir Arthur Salter, Vera Brittain, Storm Jameson, and J. Middleton Murray were members of the Peace Pledge Union.[142]

[136] Devere Allen, "Giving War the Straight Arm," *The World Tomorrow,* X (February, 1927), 73; Allen, *Fight for Peace,* p. 609; Martin, *Pacifism,* p. 142.

[137] Aldous Leonard Huxley, *Encyclopaedia of Pacifism* (New York: Harper and Brothers, 1937), p. 72. The most complete and authoritative discussion of British pacifism in the inter-war period is found in Martin, *Pacifism,* pp. 85-200.

[138] Curti, *Peace or War,* p. 272.

[139] Allen, *Fight for Peace,* p. 609.

[140] *Ibid.,* p. 617.

[141] H. C. Engelbrecht, "The Army of Men Without Hate," *The World Tomorrow,* XIII (April, 1930), 180-181.

[142] Allan Armstrong Hunter, "Will England's Pacifists Stick?" *The Christian Century,* LV (September 28, 1938), 1155; Martin, *Pacifism,* pp. 139-144.

The writers A. A. Milne and H. G. Wells, together with the philosopher C. E. M. Joad, proclaimed their pacifism. In the labor movement, George Lansbury, chairman of the Labour Party until 1935, was a Christian pacifist, as was A. Fenner Brockway, chairman of the British Independent Labour Party.

A prize acquisition to any pacifist group was a general who renounced war. The German pacifist movement had such a figure in Major General Paul Freiherr von Schoenaich, as did the French in General Percin, an artillery expert who had fought in both the Franco-Prussian War and the First World War.[143]

Albert Einstein spoke bravely as an absolute pacifist member of the War Resisters' International. In France, the novelist Romain Rolland acted as the patron saint of the French pacifists, while in Asia, two spiritual giants of the twentieth century lived and taught pacifism: Mohandas K. Gandhi and Toyohiko Kagawa, the Japanese Christian minister, labor leader, novelist, and organizer of cooperatives.

This, in short, portrays the extent and nature of pacifism during the inter-war period. It was a movement that had a renaissance between 1919 and 1941, centering in Western Europe and the United States. It was a movement most notable for its intellectual leadership. Unfortunately for it, it was also notable for its lack of unity, both in program and in organization. That it reflected a deep aspiration of human beings—the vision of a world at peace—is evident in the attraction it had for people in all walks of life, clergy, students, laborers, scholars, and, on occasion, statesmen. That it failed to win the peace was a profound tragedy for Western Civilization.

[143] Paul Freiherr von Schoenaich, "A German General Turns Pacifist," *The World Tomorrow,* XI (November, 1928), 444; *The World Tomorrow,* VII (February, 1924), 54.

CHAPTER II

PACIFISM AND THE NATURE AND CAUSES OF WAR

In the long, frightening months of 1917 the crusading fervor of the progressive spirit was transfigured by the matchless prose of Woodrow Wilson into a far-flung battle against the legions of autocracy. A war entered upon in part because of violations of neutral rights became in the minds of the people a sacred, national mission to bring the message of democracy to the world. The spirit of the day can best be recaptured by taking note once again of the words of the President:

> . . . it must be peace without victory. . . . But the right is more precious than peace, and we shall fight for the things which we have always carried nearest our hearts. . . . The world must be made safe for democracy. Its peace must be planted upon the trusted foundation of political liberty. We have no selfish ends to serve. . . . We are but one of the champions of the rights of mankind. . . .
>
> A new light shines about us. The great duties of a new day awaken a new and greater national spirit in us. We shall never again be divided or wonder what stuff we are made of. . . . America is privileged to spend her blood and her might for the principles that gave her birth and happiness and the peace which she has treasured. God helping her, she can do no other. . . .[1]

Scarcely a decade and a half later, the foremost spokesman of liberal Protestantism in the United States, perhaps the first among the popular preachers of that time, pronounced this bitter judgment:

> I renounce war because of what it does to our men. I've seen it. I renounce it because of what it forces us to do to the enemy. I renounce and will not sanction it because of its consequences and the undying hatred it nourishes. I renounce it and never again will I be in another war.
>
> I stimulated raiding parties to their murderous tasks. Do you see why I want to make it personal? I lied to the Unknown Soldier about a possible good consequence of the war. There are times I don't want to believe in immortality—the times I want to think that the Unknown Soldier can never realize how fruitless was his effort. The support I gave to war is a deep condemnation upon my soul. . . .
>
> The noblest qualities of human life, which could make earth a heaven, make it, in war, a hell. Men cannot have Christ and war at the same time. I renounce war.[2]

[1] Woodrow Wilson, *President Wilson's State Papers and Addresses.* Edited by Albert Shaw (New York: George H. Doran, 1918), pp. 352, 381, 382-383, 433.

[2] Harry Emerson Fosdick as quoted in Oswald Garrison Villard, "Dr. Fosdick Renounces War," *The Nation,* CXXXVIII (May 23, 1934), 581.

Dr. Harry Emerson Fosdick was not alone in his disillusionment. The new spirit appeared in unwonted places. Three years earlier in September, 1931, the Thomas Jefferson Post No. 310 of the American Legion in Detroit, Michigan, upon hearing an address by Methodist Bishop Paul Jones, petitioned the President of the United States to put an end immediately to all expenditures for our armed forces other than what was necessary for the exercise of the domestic police power.[3] In Stamford, Ontario, three hundred Canadian veterans, stripping from their old uniforms their victory medals, sent to each of the twenty-one combatant nations of the Great War this terse message with one of the discarded medals: "The victory emblems we surrender, one to each nation, are to be melted down with all the other rewards of armed conflict."[4] In the early spring of 1935, on the night before the American fleet sailed for war maneuvers in the north Pacific, Protestant ministers and Jewish rabbis processing in the Riverside Church in New York bore the Cross and the Star of David together for perhaps the first time in history to symbolize their united protest. Over two hundred clergymen and hundreds of laymen vowed that night: "In loyalty to God, I believe the way of true religion cannot be reconciled with the way of war."[5]

The American people had tried in 1917-1918 to follow Wilson to the heights of Sinai but on the march they lost their leader and for two decades they trekked through a wilderness of despair and disillusionment. To a later generation it is well-nigh impossible to recapture the spirit of the twenties and the thirties—partly, no doubt, because it was a reaction to the naive youthful idealism of the war years with its conviction that democracy, justice, and peace were, once and for all, to replace war. The bitterness of the reaction was a reflection of the intensity of their idealism.

A swift glance at the troubles of the twenties and thirties might help us to understand the origin and growth of that phenomenon which may be termed the "doctrine of the First World War." The failure of the peace conference to bring forth the utopia imaged in the American mind, to some the rejection of the League of Nations treaty by the Senate, and the unending turbulence of the succeeding decades resulted in the formation of the doctrine that war is an absolute evil and that the troublous events of the inter-war period were the natural, inevitable products of any and all wars.

The conclusion of the Great Crusade did not bring domestic peace to the United States. Under the cover of a seemingly boundless prosperity and amazing technological advances, there appeared disturbing

[3] *The Christian Century,* XLVIII (October 7, 1931), 1228.
[4] *The Christian Century,* L (December 27, 1933), 1629.
[5] *The Christian Century,* LII (May 15, 1935), 627, 669.

challenges to the vital fibre of the democracy: violent labor unrest in the coal and textile industries, Palmer's "red-hunt" and a narrowing interpretation of civil rights by the Supreme Court, the Sacco-Vanzetti case, gangsterism, race riots, the cancerous growth of the Ku Klux Klan, the Teapot Dome affair, the unrest of the farmers. To sensitive idealists these were indeed ". . . years of tragic disillusionment."[6] The "revolt" of the youth, the jazz craze, the cult of Freud, behaviorism, and scientific materialism, the novels of Fitzgerald, Hemingway, and Dos Passos: all seemed to spell the negation of human values and the death-toll of the American dream. In world affairs the United States strove to secure the advantages of peace without the essential corollary of responsibility.

Then came the Great Depression and the "doctrine of the First World War" was vigorously expanded to encompass the new tragedy. The banker and the financier became scapegoats for the whole business of war, revitalizing an old progressive doctrine that war is brought about by the desires and machinations of the banker, the industrialist, and the munitions maker. The challenge of the depression welded together once again the scattered strands of progressivism and the movement was brought to a culmination in the social and the economic legislation of the New Deal. As hope once again infused the democracy, however, the fragile peace structure collapsed throughout the world. Again the First World War loomed large in the minds of Americans as they saw in Manchuria, Ethiopia, Spain, the Anti-Comintern Pact, Austria, and Munich the last crowning tragedies of Wilson's War.

The supreme disaster was that Hitler and Mussolini faced ". . . an overwhelming majority of the people of the world, with unrivaled resources and technology and a great superiority in military and naval power unable to curb aggression because unwilling to run the risk of war."[7] The "doctrine of the First World War" had done its work well. In the United States the doctrine joined hands with the old American tradition of a ". . . feeling of apartness coupled with a belief in the degeneracy of Europe and the unique virtue of American institutions and motives. . . ."[8] The fruit of the alliance was isolationism with its Nye Committee and neutrality legislation. Like the people of the European democracies, Americans sought every means possible to avoid the evil of war. In bitterness and disdain they hurled at the memory of Woodrow Wilson the lofty phrases he had penned in 1917. Norman Thomas in

[6] Norman Thomas, "Can Pacifism Act Against Injustice?" *The World Tomorrow,* VII (July, 1924), 210.

[7] Arthur Stanley Link, *American Epoch: A History of the United States Since the 1890's* (New York: Alfred A. Knopf, 1953), p. 447. (Hereinafter cited as Link, *American Epoch.*)

[8] *Ibid.,* p. 463.

1937 said, "Moreover a declaration of war in capitalist America would not initiate a new struggle to make the world safe for democracy any more truly than . . . April 6, 1917."[9] Ernest Fremont Tittle in 1941 phrased his dejection; "The world was not made safe for democracy or for morality or for Christianity or for anything else that decent men care for. . . ."[10] Oswald Garrison Villard added his judgment on Wilson: "Many pacifists whom I know have today not merely contempt for Woodrow Wilson; they also have a profound conviction of his absolute stupidity in 1917 and of his utter ignorance of the forces with which he was dealing, which made a catspaw of him."[11]

No group in the United States presented a more comprehensive exposition of the "doctrine of the First World War" than did the pacifists. It was not that they had a distinctive interpretation to add to it; in all essentials they expressed thoughts shared alike by the revisionists, the disillusioned, and the isolationists. The pacifist, however, from the very nature of his position, had constantly to turn over in his mind the problem of war and peace. He was on the alert for every idea, for every piece of evidence that would incriminate the war system and justify his refusal to participate. Thus an analysis of pacifist thought in the inter-war period provides a full statement of the anti-war thought of that era. We will turn first to the pacifist's picture of the nature of the war system.

Quincy Wright in his massive study on war defines war as ". . . the legal condition which equally permits two or more hostile groups to carry on a conflict by armed force."[12] The pacifists never achieved such a precise nor limited definition. They spoke vaguely of war as a method or system, a social institution which encompassed both the causes of and preparations for conflict, and the consequences of the conflict. War became, in their hands, an all-inclusive term covering anything or everything they disliked or feared. It was not force or conflict that the pacifists were protesting against generally, but the war system as a whole because it was anarchic, unrestrained by any body of law. Few pacifists, for example, opposed the exercise of the police power by the state or local government; many pacifists supported the idea of establishing an international police force to be regulated by international law. The war system employed force without restraint,

[9] Norman Thomas, "The Pacifist's Dilemma," *The Nation,* CXLIV (January 16, 1937), 67.

[10] Ernest Fremont Tittle, "If America Is Drawn into War, Can You, as a Christian, Participate in It or Support It?" *The Christian Century,* LVIII (February 5, 1941), 178.

[11] Oswald Garrison Villard, "Retrospect," *The Nation,* CXLVI (April 2, 1938), 388.

[12] Quincy Wright, *A Study of War,* 2 volumes (Chicago: University of Chicago Press, 1942), I, 13.

without rational control; it permeated all of life with indiscriminate suffering placed upon the innocent as well as the guilty. To pacifists, who were for the most part idealists, liberal perfectionists, war was a disease, a social abnormality which needed but a correct diagnosis and a forceful appeal to the reason of men to effect its cure.

The pacifist's description of the nature of the war system resembles the abolitionist's description of slavery. Assuming that war was evil, sinful, or immoral, the pacifist developed a series of phrases to express the assumption in specific terms. There was little attempt at a logical analysis or proof of these statements; they were handed out as self-evident truths. The statements were absolute, final; their origins were indistinct, perhaps deeply rooted in personal experience or feeling. The phrases were by no means entirely new but the experience of the First World War gave them a fresh relevance and vitality they had never had before. Henry Rutgers Marshall, in the midst of the First World War, could state that war was the greatest of evils, that war breeds worse wars, and that few wars ever accomplish the purpose for which they were waged.[13] Such ideas have been the common stock of humanity for generations but in the decades of the twenties and thirties they took on a new significance. Seldom were the phrases documented with reference to specific historical experience except for general allusions such as ". . . the Great War tells us . . .," or, ". . . the First World War proves. . . ." This would seem to indicate that the ideas did not need proof to convince the popular mind; the primary assumption that all had experienced the First World War was sufficient evidence for the validity of the statement.

The pacifists were seeking neither historical nor scientific truth; their purpose was didactic and moralistic. They hoped to achieve, through a constant repetition of the phrases, a mass abhorrence of war. They envisioned a public state of mind that would make another war an impossibility. There was always a prophetic tinge to their statements. Not only were they describing a self-evident truth about war in the past; they were issuing warnings of what the future held if ever man should have recourse to war again.

Traditionally pacifist thought had appealed to the religious or moral convictions of men. This appeal was forcefully reasserted in the inter-war period but new emphases appeared as well. The appeal to utilitarian values and to common-sense reason, assumed a large role in their thought. A third appeal, the appeal to fear, appears to have permeated the whole body of pacifist thought. It is difficult to measure the extent to which it motivated or characterized this thought, but its role was not insignificant.

[13] Henry Rutgers Marshall, "The Pacifist at War," *The Atlantic Monthly*, CXXI (May, 1918), 665.

The articulators of the pacifist position in the inter-war period presented a well-rounded or complex description of the nature of the war system; they were not satisfied with a single generalization or one type of appeal. Above all else they stated their truths with confidence, with the authority and righteous conviction of new converts. Deceived by the First World War, as most of them had been, they were the heralds of a new "realism" which, in truth, was but the eternal Utopia they were forever pursuing. There were five major aspects of their understanding of the nature of war.

(1) *War as Sin—An Appeal to Conscience.* "War is Sin! War is hell! War is organized atrocity! . . ."[14] was a constant refrain in the writings of the liberal Protestants whose thought dominated the pacifist movement of the day. The ceaseless repetition of the idea of war as the ". . . sum of all villainies. . . ."[15] led Ernest Tittle to proclaim, "Has any other institution in history ever come as near to a genuine repentance as the church has in respect of her attitude toward war? Today, certainly, the church has no illusions as to the character of war."[16] Tittle's statement offers a clue to the impressive influx of Protestant ministers into the pacifist ranks. Their recollections of the First World War were particularly bitter for as leaders in public life they had delivered the church into the hands of the state, echoing the war cry, at times in its most hysterical and chauvinistic tones. But the war had not brought the promised peace, the promised rule of justice, and the Protestant ministers, at least the liberal element, stood condemned in their own eyes for having put their trust in less than holy means. Never again, they vowed, would they be deceived by war. They drew up a lengthy list of charges that established the sinfulness of the war system. Some found new validity in the age-old commandment forbidding killing. More specifically, it was the indiscriminate killing of the innocent with the guilty that disturbed the conscience of this generation. The slaughter of civilian populations, the robbery, torture, and suffering of the masses, provided the most telling religious and moral attack that could be made on the war system. It was this factor that led a few Catholics, for example, into the pacifist ranks, for the killing of the innocent violated a basic qualification in the Catholic definition of a "just" war.[17] War, moreover, was sin because it vio-

[14] Donovan E. Smucker to the Editors of *The Nation, The Nation,* CXLIX (September 16, 1939), 303.

[15] Oswald Garrison Villard, "Valedictory," *The Nation,* CL (June 29, 1940), 782.

[16] Ernest Fremont Tittle, "Preaching and Practicing Peace," *The Christian Century,* LII (April 3, 1935), 443.

[17] "The Problem of Pacifism," *The Commonweal,* XIII (April 29, 1931), 701-702; Benjamin Francis Musser, "On Poetry and War," *The Catholic World,* CXXXIX (September, 1934), 705-706.

lated or destroyed the personality—the qualities that distinguish the human from the animal. War made automatons or machines of men; it forbade feeling or thinking. Worse even than killing was the breeding of hatred. In Quaker thought this meant the violation or destruction of the divine image in man.[18] Furthermore, war involved the distortion of truth; it rested on a propaganda of lies, fear, and hatred. Here again the attack hit home. To the popular conviction that the United States had been led into the war by the bold deceptions of an Allied propaganda mill, the pacifists lent their support and their condemnation of propaganda as one of the evils that had misled them in 1917. They now treated it with self-conscious suspicion. Basic was the conviction of the pacifists that they had betrayed themselves into the use of unholy means to achieve a holy end and thus they were realizing in their experience the truth of the moral that you cannot fight evil with evil and expect good to come of it. That the end does not justify the means is the implicit message of the appeal to conscience.

Moving in the spirit of the social gospel movement, there was a refreshing sense among the Protestant pacifists that once again they had discovered the early Christian faith, the living church of the first century. They affirmed with confidence that God was an eternal loving Spirit. With the God of Love triumphant it was not difficult to condemn killing, hatred, oppression, and, therefore, war as evil. Too, the liberal Protestant pacifists rediscovered that Jesus was a pacifist. The assertion of faith in Jesus as the source and justification for their pacifism was always accompanied by the remembrance of the warrior they had made of Him during the war. They recalled such bellicose utterances as that of Joseph Odell in 1918: "He set His face steadfastly, marched forward with eyes unafraid, and finally flung Himself upon the munitions of His enemies in a great abandon of passion. . . . No one has ever outranked Him in manhood, heroism, fortitude."[19] In reaction the pacifists spoke of a universal Christ who had no place whatsoever on the battlefield. To give practical expression to their movement in taking Christ out of uniform pacifist ministers pledged never to serve as chaplains. In an Armistice Day address, Fosdick explained the process of rationalization whereby men faced with the terror of war make of it a sacred cause in order to justify their complicity.[20]

The cross too became a symbol of pacifism, the highest expression

[18] David Elton Trueblood, "The Renunciation of Hatred," *The Christian Century,* LIII (April 15, 1936), 563.

[19] Joseph H. Odell, "Peter Sat by the Fire Warming Himself," *The Atlantic Monthly*, CXXI (February, 1918), 149, 150.

[20] Harry Emerson Fosdick, "Putting Christ into Uniform," *The Christian Century,* LVI (December 13, 1939), 1539.

of nonresistance. Allan Hunter caught this human identification with the cross in his statement that Jesus would gladly face a machine gun but he would never aim one at the Germans.[21] The pacifists now understood that the method of Jesus in bringing about His Kingdom of peace and justice was that of love and nonviolence. In the 1939 Declaration of Reaffirmation of Pacifist Faith, signed by over one thousand Protestant ministers, were these words: "Nonviolent, forgiving love alone reconciles man to God and man to man . . . we call upon the church to enter into deeper fellowship with that church which refused to serve in Caesar's armies. . . ."[22] Faith in the establishment of a just and peaceable Kingdom on this earth was not destroyed by the war; rather, the method of achieving it had been purified. The confidence of the liberal Protestant pacifists in the social gospel, far from being shattered by the war experience, took on new meaning and courage because it was now felt that they had discovered their source of earlier weakness. In pacifism, not understood simply as a protest against war, but as an attitude to be applied to all the social relationships of life, they felt they had found the key to the Kingdom, the means to win the peace and realize the society in which all men would be brothers. The strength of their conviction was witnessed to by the tenacity with which they held to their pacifism right up to Pearl Harbor, through years when it was a far from easy matter to sustain a pacifist faith with Hitler challenging their devotion to justice.

The pacifism of the liberal Protestants met with strong criticism. While praising the courage of their stand and the need for the testimony of ideal love in the world, opponents were quick to point out what they believed to be misplaced emphases and diluted theology in their thought. Catholic writers asserted the natural right of man to self-preservation as God-given. From this they argued that defensive war was just and it was a strict duty of citizenship to support such a war. Killing, they pointed out, was not always murder; the police power of the state, for example, involved the killing of those who endangered the maintenance of order in society.[23] Charles Clayton Morrison, the editor of *The Christian Century,* charged the pacifists with confusing cause and effect. War, he said, was neither moral nor immoral, but amoral. It was a final appeal to might, a state not subject to ethical judgment. War was a tragedy; it was a moral predicament in

[21] Allan Armstrong Hunter, "Pacifists and the United Front," *The Christian Century,* LIII (January 8, 1936), 48.

[22] "Christian Pacifists Take Their Stand," *The Christian Century,* LVI (March 15, 1939), 344-345.

[23] Joseph Keating, "The Right of Self-Preservation," *The Catholic World,* CXLIV (November, 1936), 234-236; "The Problem of Pacifism," *The Commonweal,* XIII (April 29, 1931), 701-702; "No Sword Is So Keen," *The Commonweal,* XXI (January 11, 1935), 299-300.

which men have lost their freedom to choose between right and wrong. To be nonresistant in modern war when there is no conceivable way of avoiding participation in the war save by death was ". . . spitting in the wind of ineluctable reality."[24] The judgment of evil must rest, not on war, but on the causes that produced the war, the injustices that brought to pass the tragedy. In war Morrison found the judgment of God for man's disobedience.[25]

The most forceful critic of the Protestant pacifists was Reinhold Niebuhr. There was a touch of irony in this for Niebuhr was a fellow pacifist until the early thirties. His charge was leveled at their absolutist creed and their liberal theology. Niebuhr saw that the best that men could strive for in life was a measure of justice. Justice was a relative thing, a compromise in response to possible historical alternatives always less than ideal. The liberal Protestant's optimistic faith in progress and perfectionism failed to grasp the reality of the complexity of human nature. Pacifism, Niebuhr believed, which ". . . springs from an unholy compound of gospel perfectionism and bourgeois utopianism, the latter having had its rise in eighteenth century rationalism . . .,[26] is always a source of confusion in dealing with immediate issues, because it accelerates the evils encountered by comparing them with a perfection which history does not know.[27]

The ethical appeal to conscience was a restatement of the "sins" enumerated above in general humanist terms. The sin of violating the commandment against killing, for example, was stated ethically as: murder is immoral. Einstein used this term when he said that he found the murder of men to be disgusting.[28] Ethical judgments on war emphasized the cruelty and ruthlessness of war. Time and time again documents such as the army instruction manual for bayonet practice were quoted to unmask war as the denial of human values. The most disturbing problem of war to the ethical approach, as to the religious, was that posed by modern technology which made possible the scientific

[24] Charles Clayton Morrison, "The War as Tragedy," *The Christian Century,* LIX (January 7, 1942), 8.

[25] *Ibid.,* 6-8.

[26] Reinhold Niebuhr, "If America Is Drawn into War, Can You, as a Christian, Participate in It or Support It?" *The Christian Century,* LVII (December 18, 1940), 1580.

[27] Reinhold Niebuhr, "Idealists As Cynics," *The Nation,* CL (January 20, 1940), 73; see also: Reinhold Niebuhr, "Must We Do Nothing," *The Christian Century,* XLIX (March 30, 1932), 415-417; Reinhold Niebuhr, "Must Democracy Use Force? II. Peace and the Liberal Illusion," *The Nation,* CXLVIII (January 28, 1939), 117-119; Reinhold Niebuhr, "An End to Illusions," *The Nation,* CL (June 29, 1940), 778-779.

[28] Albert Einstein as quoted in Paul Hutchinson, "Einstein and the Red Flag," *The Christian Century,* XLVI (August 28, 1929), 1056.

slaughter of civilians as well as combatants. These new weapons seemed to justify the sweeping ethical condemnation of war as immoral.

(2) *War as Technology—An Appeal to Fear.* The German general, Paul Freiherr von Schoenaich, converted to pacifism after long service under Bismarck and the Emperor William II, denounced war on the grounds that the end to chivalry and spontaneity in armed combat rendered war intolerable.[29] This wistful desire to return to the age of knighthood was a reaction to the impersonality of modern weapons. The pacifists, who during the inter-war period deplored these weapons, though not for the same reason, continued a traditional fight against armaments, meeting every appropriation bill calling for increases in spending for the army, navy, or air force with a full barrage of their own propaganda. It was the naval program that especially nettled the pacifist because of the competition such building inspired.

Of more importance to understanding pacifist thought, however, were the repeated references to weapons or techniques made possible by modern technology that made war a nightmare to the civilian as well as the soldier. The first was poison gas, the second the aerial bomb, and the third the technique of the starvation blockade made possible by the modern navy. The relationship of these weapons to the experience of the First World War is obvious. Here too we see the prophetic element present. Every time these weapons were mentioned, they not only called to mind the experience of the past but they predicted, implicitly or explicitly, that the same weapons, or ones even more devastating, would make another war as terrifying as the last.

Why did the pacifists call these weapons to the attention of their readers? It might be expected that they had in mind a plan for international control or outlawing of these deadly weapons. The only pacifist though who seriously advanced such a program was Villard who urged the outlawing of the bomber, the submarine, poison gas, and bacteria.[30] In fact the pacifists were appealing to fear in order to create such a revulsion in the minds of men that they would never again resort to war.

(3) *War and Political Institutions—An Appeal to Fear.* The propensity of the pacifist mind to generalize and to create absolutes indiscriminately is nowhere better revealed than in its attempt to understand the interaction of war and political institutions. The immediate basis for this was the experience of the First World War and the years immediately following which saw extensive government controls over

[29] Paul Freiherr von Schoenaich, "German Pacifism During the War," *The Nation*, CXXVII (November 7, 1928), 482-483.

[30] Oswald Garrison Villard, "Issues and Men," *The Nation*, CXLVII (July 2, 1938), 18.

industry, communications, and business relations, censorship of the sources of public information, the Espionage and Sedition Acts, and the deep inroads made upon traditional concepts of civil liberty in the anti-German hysteria of the war and the "red-scare" in the years following which culminated in the infamous Palmer raid on New Year's Day, 1920. From this experience and the supporting evidence mustered from past wars, the pacifists generalized freely, and, most significantly, prophesied the future in the darkest of hues.

In October, 1929, *The Christian Century* published a story entitled "A War Time Memory," which was the account of three pacifist ministers in California who had been arrested and convicted for conducting a pacifist meeting back in October, 1917.[31] The appearance of this article in 1929 was not without significance, for on May 27 of that year Madame Rosika Schwimmer, a veteran pacifist crusader, was denied citizenship by the Supreme Court for her refusal to take an oath to bear arms in defense of the country.[32] Justice Holmes entered one of his incisive dissents touched with a biting irony: "I would suggest that the Quakers have done their share to make the country what it is, that many citizens agree with the applicant's belief and that I had not supposed hitherto that we regretted our inability to expel them because they believe more than some of us do in the teachings of the Sermon on the Mount."[33] During 1930 and 1931 the Macintosh-Bland citizenship cases toured the courts until the Supreme Court finally rejected their applications for citizenship. There was not a little incongruity in the refusal to admit Dr. Douglas Macintosh, a fifty-three year old professor of theology who was not a pacifist but who wished to retain the right to decide whether a war was morally justified before he entered it as a combatant, and Marie Averill Bland, a forty-seven year old nurse who, while refusing to bear arms, offered to serve her country in any non-combative service during war.[34] Pacifists saw a great deal more than the incongruity. They saw the inroads of a war system into the peace time functions of government. Without conscious awareness of the forces involved, the pacifists were witnessing too the force of twentieth century nationalism which, as Ralph Gabriel perceived, ". . . threatened every other doctrine

[31] Robert Whitaker, "A War Time Memory," *The Christian Century,* XLVI (October 30, 1929), 1338-1340.

[32] "Justice Holmes and the Schwimmer Case," *The New Republic,* LIX (June 12, 1929), 92-93; *The Nation,* CXXVIII (June 12, 1929), 689; Dorothy Dunbar Bromley, "The Pacifist Bogey: An Apology to Prospective Citizens," *Harper's Monthly Magazine,* CLXI (October, 1930), 553-565.

[33] Justice Oliver Wendell Holmes as quoted in "Justice Holmes and the Schwimmer Case," *The New Republic,* LIX (June 12, 1929), 93.

[34] *The New Republic,* LIX (July 3, 1929), 164; *The Nation,* CXXXI (July 16, 1930), 57; *The Nation,* CXXXII (June 3, 1931), 595.

of the American democratic pattern." Nationalism, he warned, ". . . creating the Leviathan state, challenges the ideal of the free individual . . . that old belief in a fundamental law governing nations as well as men . . . the belief in a natural and moral law before which not only all men but all nation states are equal and from which men and nations derive equal and inalienable rights. . . ."[35]

The Christian Century article was an evident reminder of the danger to hallowed liberties in time of war as the citizenship cases reminded pacifists in peace time that their lot was a precarious one. The pacifists shared the memory of tortures imposed on conscientious objectors at Leavenworth and Alcatraz during the First World War and of the odium in which non-conformist minority groups were held in war time, captured so vividly in this warning of John Haynes Holmes: "The wolves of fanaticism and terror, of blind prejudice and passion, will bite with the upper teeth of the law and the lower teeth of the mob. Their fangs will rend and tear more fiercely than in the First World War."[36] Thus the pacifists entered the ranks of the defenders of civil liberties.

Upon the foundation of these experiences they constructed the doctrine that a democracy could not fight a war in the future without becoming a totalitarian state. Among the earliest expressions of this avowal in pacifist writing was one in 1937 and the doctrine continued to flourish until the United States entered the war in 1941. The time limitation indicates the source of the generalization. The rise of military dictatorships in Germany and Italy provided a new equation for pacifist thought. The war system now became synonymous with fascism; to wage war under modern conditions required a fascist organization of the state. Fascism appeared, or was made to appear, as the logical extension of the government controls of the First World War; for fascism, was interpreted by pacifists not as a political aberration, but as the end product of the capitalist economic system.

With confidence in their insight, pacifists foretold the junking of the Constitution,[37] the regimentation of the state, tyranny, and the emergence of a dictator. Contemporary events in Europe and Asia appeared to give their predictions a high degree of plausibility. The flavor of these jeremiads is found in such statements as that of Harold Bosley when he contended that war involved ". . . the tyrannical mobili-

[35] Ralph Henry Gabriel, *The Course of American Democratic Thought: An Intellectual History Since 1815* (New York: Ronald Press, 1940), p. 416. (Hereinafter cited as Gabriel, *American Democratic Thought.*)

[36] John Haynes Holmes, "A Pacifist Minister to His Brethren," *The Christian Century,* LVI (November 8, 1939), 1374.

[37] Thomas F. Doyle, "To War or Not to War?" *The Catholic World,* CL (December, 1939), 266.

zation of mental, spiritual and material resources."[38] Bertrand Russell, early in 1939, predicted that if England entered the war she would have to become "cruel" and "hysterical" like the Nazis.[39] It is surprising that the example of British democracy in the early years of the Second World War did not quiet the fears of Americans, yet the predictions kept coming. Albert Palmer in 1941 set forth the dogma: "War and even thorough-going preparation means embracing fascism, at least for the duration of the war."[40] Fosdick in the same year said, "After every world war, whoever wins it, there is bound to be less democracy than there was before. . . ."[41]

These statements indicated a distrust of the survival power of democracy, of political institutions that had persisted despite many wars in the past. Villard gave a hint as to the source of the distrust in his statement that war ". . . will inevitably end all social and political progress, lower still further the standard of living, enslave labor, and, if persisted in, impose a dictatorship and turn us into a totalitarian state."[42] The appeal of the pacifists thus was not alone to the belief in the ". . . unique virtue of American institutions and motives . . .,"[43] but to the vital stake the American people had in the political, social, and economic experiments of the New Deal. The explanation of the distrust in the ability of our democracy to survive another war would seem to be explained in part as a reaction to the Great Depression. They saw that the war threatened to interrupt and, most likely, destroy the erection of the new structure of progressive legislation which still seemed to be in its fragile infancy. It is this that explains the pacifist corollary that the responsibility of the United States was to stay aloof from the war, preserve and perfect her democracy, and thus maintain civilization until the end of the war when she could distribute her gifts and graces to the tattered nations of Europe. This mixture of devotion to the democratic ideal with self-righteousness and self-interest became a part of the pacifist political creed. In this light the following statement becomes meaningful: "The ultimate justification of America's abstention from the war lies in the hope that by conserving its democratic

[38] Harold Bosley, "Illusions of the Disillusioned," *The Christian Century,* LVIII (January 1, 1941), 14.

[39] Bertrand Russell, "Must Democracy Use Force? III. Munich Rather Than Force," *The Nation,* CXLVIII (February 11, 1939), 174.

[40] Albert W. Palmer, "If America Is Drawn into War, Can You, As a Christian, Participate in It or Support It?" *The Christian Century,* LVIII (January 8, 1941), 52.

[41] Harry Emerson Fosdick, "If America Is Drawn into War, Can You, As a Christian, Participate in It or Support It?" *The Christian Century,* LVIII (January 22, 1941), 117.

[42] Oswald Garrison Villard, "Valedictory," *The Nation,* CL (June 29, 1940), 782.

[43] Link, *American Epoch,* p. 463.

integrity, its moral and material strength, and its spiritual resources, this country may be able to render service in the name of civilization to the nations, both vanquished and victors, which a prolonged war will leave prostrate."[44] No explanation was given to explain how a nation unwilling to assume its share of responsibility for the world political situation would suddenly become, upon the conclusion of the war, the humane servant of all nations in the name of civilization. Thus by appealing to the fear of a militaristic totalitarian state in the event of war and the fear that material and social progress would come to a halt or be destroyed, the pacifists added another block to the edifice of revulsion against war that they were creating in the minds of men.

(4) *War and Psychological and Social Factors—An Appeal to Fear.* The liberals and the social gospel ministers, who dominated almost completely the expression of pacifist thought, shared a common faith in progress, a belief that men through proper education, democratic institutions, and scientific legislation would frame an ever more perfect social order. Suffering, crime, and poverty were diseases of society needing only proper diagnosis and social action to effect their cure. This faith rested on the assumption that the common man is not only capable, but worthy of participating in and ultimately controlling the democratic process by which progress takes place. Yet, as already noted, these same groups despaired of democratic institutions surviving another war. Another evidence of their distrust was found in their great fear of propaganda. Here again the First World War reminded them forcefully of the power of this weapon which they believed destroyed the reasonableness of the people and placed them submissively in the hands of government. The doctrine that America was led into the World War through the clever wiles of Allied propaganda was not accepted by all pacifists, but by a large enough segment to give it a firm place in their thought. In the June, 1923, issue of *The World Tomorrow,* devoted entirely to a consideration of propaganda, Robert Morss Lovett attributed to propaganda the power to ". . . manufacture victories for home consumption and invent a mythology of war aims for use abroad."[45]

The pacifists saw that propaganda, a word they used to mean the deliberate distortion of truth, created fear, suspicion, and hatred. Ernest L. Meyer, a conscientious objector in the First World War, testified to the power of propaganda in molding public opinion to the point where the pressure on the non-conformist became unbearable. This pressure ". . . made one feel as an alien in a world of strangers,

[44] "The Church in Wartime," *The Christian Century,* LVI (December 13, 1939), 1536.

[45] Robert Morss Lovett, "The Pitfalls of Propaganda," *The World Tomorrow,* VI (June, 1923), 167.

or as a madman in an institution wherein all others are accredited as sane."[46] The deeper problem of the relationship between the liberal democratic faith and the implications of the anti-intellectualism of the new psychology and sociology was either unrecognized or ignored. This appeal to the fear of being deceived through propaganda contributed to the hesitancy of Americans in the thirties to recognize the threat that Hitler and Mussolini posed to the peace structure and to the survival of democracy.

Another psychological factor that deeply distressed the pacifists was the attraction war has always had for men—the call to courage, heroism, adventure, sacrifice, and honor. Every time war beckoned, it found the willing response of men. The pacifists never found a substitute, a "moral equivalent for war"; they rested their hopes on the horrors and impersonality of modern combat as a deterrent to the call of the state.

As to the implications of war for the social structure and social institutions, the pacifists failed to develop their formulation of doctrine in this area to any appreciable extent. Donovan Smucker proposed that war was anti-labor but he failed to develop his argument.[47] Tittle believed that war provided a "field-day" for the jingo press, for an unsavory band of politicians, and for "anti-social" industries such as munitions-making.[48] Henry Huizinga, speaking out of his experience as a missionary in China, foresaw a generation of orphans and refugees as the fruit of war.[49] He did not envision the mass migrations of homeless people following the Second World War, but he was aware of this social consequence of war so tragic in its implications.

(5) *War and Utility—An Appeal to Reason and the Pocketbook.* The pacifist's appeal to reason and the pocketbook emphasized the incredible waste to life and property that war brought—the unbelievable fact that men could ". . . spend billions of dollars and sacrifice thousands of lives. . . ."[50] for the elusive harvest of war. Using the impressive statistics Ernest Bogart had compiled on the Great War,[51] the

[46] Ernest L. Meyer, "If War Should Come and I'd Refuse," *The Christian Century,* XLIX (September 28, 1932), 1163.

[47] Donovan E. Smucker to the Editors of *The Nation,* September 6, 1939, *The Nation,* CXLIX (September 16, 1939), 303.

[48] Ernest Fremont Tittle, "If America Is Drawn into War, Can You, as a Christian, Participate in It or Support It?" *The Christian Century,* LVIII (February 5, 1941), 178.

[49] Henry Huizinga to the Editor of *The Christian Century, The Christian Century,* LVI (January 4, 1939), 28.

[50] Kirby Page, "A New National Preparedness," *The Forum,* LXXXI (February, 1929), 74.

[51] Ernest Ludlow Bogart, *Direct and Indirect Causes of the Great War* (New York: Oxford University Press, 1919) (No. 24 in *Preliminary Economic Studies of the War,* Carnegie Endowment for International Peace, Edited by David Kinley.)

pacifists spoke in terms of debts and taxes, the destruction of property, the inordinate demands upon exhaustible natural resources, and the specter of financial ruin, national bankruptcy, and depression. Sherwood Eddy, Oswald Garrison Villard, and Thomas Doyle discerned in the depression the inevitable outcome of war—another example of the tendency to hasty and oversimplified generalization.[52] This appeal was directed not alone at the waste and cost of war, but at the expense of maintaining the war machine in peace time. Here was implied the idea that every dollar spent for defense or war meant one dollar less for economic and social progress. Characteristic of much of the pacifist doctrine, these statements received a ready assent but they rarely deterred action.

The second appeal to reason, or actually to the common sense sort of reason, was that which stressed that war never accomplishes the purpose or purposes for which it is begun; in fact, it achieves nothing save destruction, waste, and terror. We find, in support of this appeal, not a documented or analytical discussion, but short, suggestive phrases and words. The pacifist dismissed war as "stupid," "futile," "the supreme assinity;"[53] or as Villard put it, ". . . people are aware that our going to war . . . was a useless crime against America, that we got nothing out of it but misery, and that it nearly ruined the Republic we love."[54] To pronounce sentence on all war as "stupid" or "futile" may sound strange to those recalling the American Revolution, but the disillusioned were not disposed to delve deeply into their history books.

A look at the pacifist's list of things that the war did not solve brought to light Wilson's magic phrases once again, but now encumbered with incriminating negatives. War did not bring peace, did not make the world safe for democracy, did not end war, did not check evil, did not save Christianity or morality, did not bring liberty, justice, security, did not reform evildoers. The events of the twenties and thirties brought a quick, though often superficial, confirmation of the "truth" of these phrases: Versailles, Manchuria, Munich, Poland spoke volumes about the "failure" of the First World War.

A "new wisdom" about war developed in the pacifist ranks—a "wisdom" that was little more than a haphazard conglomeration of old maxims. A. J. Muste compared war with fighting on a slippery inclined plane where eventually all ended up at the bottom and it made

[52] Sherwood Eddy, "Must We Face the War Problem Again?" *The Christian Century,* LV (November 9, 1938), 1363; Oswald Garrison Villard, "Issues and Men," *The Nation,* CXLVIII (January 14, 1939), 67; Thomas F. Doyle, "To War or Not to War?" *The Catholic World,* CL (December, 1939), 274.

[53] Vernon Nash, "If All Wars or None, Then None!" *The Christian Century,* XLVIII (November 11, 1931), 1415.

[54] Oswald Garrison Villard, "Dr. Fosdick Renounces War," *The Nation,* CXXXVIII (May 23, 1934), 581.

little difference who was on the top of the pile.[55] The "new wisdom" affirmed the moral that those who take the sword perish by the sword. Bertrand Russell expressed a rationalist's despair of war; it forced a nation (thinking, of course, of Great Britain) to descend to the level of its opponent in order to conquer him, which is hardly a reasonable course of action.[56] Rockwell Kent found war an annoyance and a burden, ". . . abhorrent to the artist's soul . . ." because it represented disorder and "unseemliness."[57] Roland Bainton interpreted the futility of modern war as arising from the fact that modern technology and the economic interdependence of the nations made victory impossible and loss for all concerned inevitable.[58] Even if war should accomplish some good ". . . the evils it brings in its train, more than cancel this benefit."[59] These statements were readily assented to in peace time, but the pacifists had only touched the surface of conviction. The profound irrationality of men, nations, and life escaped them. No moral, esthetic, nor psychological equivalent of war emerged from their thought to stir the imaginations of men.

It was more difficult to envisage peace than to describe the nature of war. The pacifist often took the less difficult road of making men fear war rather than creating an active love of peace. His thought was so captivated by the memory of the First World War and his premonition of the coming of the second one that he snatched at anything resembling peace. His peace plans, as we shall see later on, were directed more at the elimination of the causes of war as he understood them than at the fulfillment of a vision of peace and at the instilling of a love of peace in men.

The criticism of the pacifist's picture of the nature of war grew apace as Hitler rose to power in Europe. By making war an absolute evil, it was charged that the pacifists had suspended their judgment on questions of honor, justice, responsibility, and practical political realities. The pacifists desired to condemn Hitler and they did, but their pacifism led them into the uncomfortable surroundings of isolationism, neutrality, and the nationalism that accompanied these policies. Bitter critics like Reinhold Niebuhr, Aurel Kolnai, and Lewis Mumford charged them with abandoning civilization at a time of crisis for an

[55] A. J. Muste to the Editor of *The Christian Century, The Christian Century,* LVII (September 11, 1940), 1116.

[56] Bertrand Russell, "Must Democracy Use Force? III. Munich Rather Than War," *The Nation,* CXLVIII (February 11, 1939), 174.

[57] Rockwell Kent, "The Artist and World Friendship," *The World Tomorrow,* VII (February, 1924), 47.

[58] Roland Bainton, "Technology and Pacifism," *The Christian Century,* LV (May 18, 1938), 618-619.

[59] Henry Joel Cadbury, "The Christian Verdict on War," *The World Tomorrow,* V (January, 1922), 16.

absolutistic creed that had no historical reality. Kolnai asserted that, after all, the opposite side of the coin of their picture of war was true also: war had settled many problems; peace bred evils; the cause of injustice triumphed in peace unless someone was willing to fight it; and it did make a great deal of difference who won a war.[60] The critics asserted that fascism meant slavery, tyranny, and the end to moral values and human personality. Years before in the midst of the devastating Civil War, President Lincoln, in a letter to a Quaker correspondent, spoke of the dilemma of the pacifist: "Your people—the Friends—have had, and are having, a very great trial. On principle, and faith, opposed to both war and oppression, they can only practically oppose oppression by war. In this hard dilemma, some have chosen one horn and some the other."[61] This same choice faced the pacifist as the world went to war a second time.

The pacifist's abiding concern with the problem of war led him to explore many possible interpretations of the causes of war. In his statement of causation, the pacifist appeared to accept indiscriminately any or all of the current theories without attempting to integrate or relate them to each other. A ready disposition to move from one opinion to the next is discernible from 1919 to 1941. Nevertheless, the variety and the vitality of his thought characterize him as one thoroughly apprised of contemporary thought about the causes of war. The pacifist's thinking bears a striking correlation to contemporary historical and philosophical trends. The pacifist, in the past often accused of being behind the times, was notably in step during the inter-war period.

The "conspiracy theory" or "blundering statesman theory" of war found few proponents, however, despite the Versailles Peace Conference and the Nye Committee investigation. One who did vigorously maintain this tradition, however, was Oswald Garrison Villard. His basic assumption was that the common people, the masses, desired peace at all times. Therefore if war came, it must have been brought on by special interest groups, or by short-sighted statesmen. Villard did not confine himself to one villain; he scattered his blows very generously. In doing so he reflected an old progressive tradition on war causation.[62] To his demeaning attack against Wilson might be added onslaughts upon Lansing, House, and J. P. Morgan and Company, the aforementioned comprising a quadrumvirate which led the United States

[60] Aurel Kolnai, "Must Democracy Use Force? I. Pacifism Means Suicide," *The Nation,* CXLVIII (January 21, 1939), 87.

[61] Abraham Lincoln to Eliza P. Gurney, September 4, 1864, in Abraham Lincoln, *The Collected Works of Abraham Lincoln,* 8 Volumes. Edited by Roy P. Basler (New Brunswick, New Jersey: Rutgers University Press, 1953), VII, 535.

[62] Link, *American Epoch,* p. 186.

into war in 1917.[63] He had harsh words for bankers and propagandists in general.[64] And when Hitler appeared on the scene Villard once again took up the cudgel to expose and condemn the parties responsible for the rise of the dictator. In an article prepared on the occasion of Hitler's announcement of German rearmament in 1935, he lashed out at the statesmen of Europe who had failed to correct the injustices of Versailles. He attacked the militarists—or, as he graphically described them: ". . . the in-time-of-peace-prepare-for-war parrots. . . ."—for draining each country of its natural resources, and thereby lowering the standard of living and producing serious threats to the financial solvency of European nations. "As long as the professional military and naval mind continues," Villard said, "we have everlasting cant about national honor and preparing for war. . . ."[65] Villard feared as well the power of the President of the United States in matters of foreign affairs. In 1936 he accused President Roosevelt of militarizing the country; from that time on until the outbreak of the war he continued an unceasing attack on every appropriation for the military.[66] When Europe went to war in 1939, Villard explained the causes as "criminal lunacy" on the part of the dictators and ". . . incredible ineptness, weakness, and diplomatic folly. . . ." on the part of the Allied statesmen.[67] Like many of his fellow Americans he could not perceive any American responsibility either for the cause or the outcome of the new "European" conflict. In the spirit of the other statements already noted, he penned an open letter to Winston Churchill in 1938:

> Finally I must point out to you that many over here feel that we owe no higher duty to democracy, to decency, to humanity itself than to keep this country out of the next war. For we know that the day this country enters a war democracy will die here, and that there will be precious little hope of reviving it whether we win or lose. . . . we . . . still feel that if war comes to you again we can do you no better service than to stay out. You Europeans will all be bankrupt whether you win or lose. Somebody ought to be left the means to put the world together again if that is possible.[68]

A few pacifists supported these charges against persons and special interest groups. Harry Overstreet, writing in 1926, uncovered a

[63] Oswald Garrison Villard, "The War and the Pacifists," *The Nation,* CXLI (October 23, 1935), 455.

[64] *Ibid.*

[65] Oswald Garrison Villard, "Gentlemen May Cry Peace," *The Saturday Review of Literature,* XI (April 6, 1935), 606-607.

[66] Oswald Garrison Villard, "Issues and Men," *The Nation,* CXLII (April 29, 1936), 550.

[67] Oswald Garrison Villard, "Issues and Men," *The Nation,* CXLIX (September 16, 1939), 293.

[68] Oswald Garrison Villard, "Open Letter to Winston Churchill," *The Nation,* CXLVII (November 5, 1938), 480.

". . . sinister interlocking and intercommunicating system of the military and military minded."[69] Kirby Page and Allan Hunter leveled charges against the militarists also.[70] Most surprising was the small number of allegations against the munitions makers. One student pacifist indicated that he could find little incentive in fighting to make the ". . . world safe for the steel magnates and munitions manufacturers;"[71] but the rarity of this sort of expression indicated the desire of the pacifist to probe deeper. More frequent and outspoken were the attacks on British and French leadership in the late thirties. Harold Bosley in 1938 saw Hitler as ". . . the finished product of that kind of statesmanship which with blundering persistence alternately uses military bluff and exalted self-righteousness to achieve its ends."[72] That the United States might also have shared in creating a world situation that made possible the advent of the Black Shirts and the Brown Shirts generally escaped the searching eye of pacifist publicists.

The magic key employed in varying shapes and sizes by all pacifists to disclose the cause of war was the economic interpretation. Pacifists have long been accused of being naive about economic matters. Merle Curti, writing in 1936, for example, accredited the past failures of the peace movement in the United States to its overlooking or discounting the economic motivation in national policy. For his own part, Curti obviously influenced by Marxist historical criticism, suggested that war was an inherent feature of a profit-motive economy, of capitalism, and that the peace movement by aligning itself with the conservative middle-class public rather than with the labor movement was perpetuating the thing it sought to eradicate. Curti wrote, "Largely middle-class in origin and development, the peace movement early set itself against any re-ordering of society for the purpose of eliminating such causes of war as social injustices, class conflict, and the profit motive. . . . War has been functional to the capitalistic system itself. . . . Pacifists have sincerely and ardently desired peace; but they in general desired the benefits of the existing order to an even greater degree."[73] Reinhold Niebuhr made a similar charge in 1927,[74] and Gorham Munson in 1939

[69] Harry A. Overstreet, "Militarizing Our Minds," *The World Tomorrow,* IX (October, 1926), 146.

[70] Kirby Page, "A New National Preparedness," *The Forum,* LXXXI (February, 1929), 73; Allan Armstrong Hunter, "Pacifists and the United Front," *The Christian Century,* LIII (January 8, 1936), 47.

[71] Harold Seidman, "The Colleges Renounce War," *The Nation,* CXXXVI (May 17, 1933), 554.

[72] Harold Bosley, "A Defense of Radical Peace Sentiment," *The Christian Century,* LV (November 21, 1938), 1324.

[73] Merle Curti, *Peace or War: The American Struggle 1636-1936* (New York: W. W. Norton and Company, 1936), pp. 13, 308, 309.

[74] Reinhold Niebuhr, "A Critique of Pacifism," *The Atlantic Monthly,* CXXXIX (May, 1927), 640.

repeated Curti's thesis when he stated, "As a movement pacifism has been notoriously innocent of economics."[75] In fact, pacifism had largely absolved itself of this charge. A. J. Muste, writing in 1924, asserted, "The fact that nowadays almost every discussion about war soon pounces upon the economic factors, is matter for encouragement. Before the war one who dealt in economic interpretation was apt to be regarded as radical, queer, materialistic, sordid, or the like."[76] Curti's charge of pacifist naïveté on economic matters seems to hold true for the peace movement prior to the First World War. After the war it was, perhaps, still a valid criticism of the conservative peace organizations. For the pacifists, however, it was a far different story.

The economic interpretation of war dominated all other theories, while the pacifists' personal economic faiths ranged from the progressive demand for government regulation of economic life through democratic socialism to Marxism. The rejection of capitalism was a strong, though not exclusive, element of their thought. In fact the two distinctive elements of pacifist thought in the inter-war period were the radical economic interpretation of the cause of war and the new interest in relating pacifism to the labor movement, or, as it was referred to, the "class struggle"—a diversion intimately related to the preoccupation with an economic interpretation.

Pacifist publicists, as a whole, interpreted the First World War as a struggle between rival imperialisms for control of world markets, trade, raw materials, and colonies. It was in this same context of thought that the subsequent events of the inter-war period were viewed. Pacifists found in the economic interpretation a handy tool that could be made to explain all the perplexities of international life; Hitler, thus, was a product of the economic inequities imposed on Germany at Versailles. It was refreshing and reassuring to have unraveled the mystery. Peace plans could be drawn up with confidence. The interpretation of war as an expression of economic imperialism seemed to be confirmed by the first major aggressions of the thirties: Japan's penetration of Manchuria and Italy's attack on Ethiopia. But the Spanish Civil War posed serious challenges to the over-simplifications of the economic imperialism theory and for the Marxists the diplomatic maneuverings of the Soviet Union in the late thirties taxed the resources of their dialectical ingenuity to the breaking point.

The economic imperialism interpretation was shared by the whole spectrum of pacifist thought. The theory began by defining "have" and "have-not" nations with reference to such criteria as access to raw ma-

[75] Gorham Bert Munson, "The Sterility of Pacifist Economics," *The Christian Century,* LVI (April 19, 1939), 513.

[76] A. J. Muste, "American Labor and Peace," *The World Tomorrow,* VII (February, 1924), 48.

terials, to world markets, to colonies, and to credit and currency resources. The tyranny of the "have" nations as expressed in the monopoly of goods, raw materials and services, in tariff barriers, and currency restrictions which resulted in inequalities in the production and distribution of the world's goods aroused the enmity and jealousy of the "have-not" nations and led them to redress the balance through acts of aggression. Pacifists discerned a potent generator of war in the demands of foreign investors for the protection of their interests, demands which were presented to the public in the finery of national honor.[77] Americans needed only to remember their relationships with Mexico to confirm the truth of this judgment. Those who ignored the reality of these economic causes, Norman Thomas said, ". . . are like those who take their ease on the side of a volcano, content because today the sun shines and heedless of the primeval fires which are beneath them."[78]

Of more significance was the sizable group of pacifists who saw the source of war not alone in the international rivalry of nations for economic ends, but in the nature of the capitalistic economy itself. Those who went no further than the former explanation could envisage peace through the adoption of an international program with provisions for free trade, international supervision of colonial areas, the distribution of raw materials, and an international judicial system to arbitrate disputes. Those, however, who found the source of the evil in capitalism itself committed themselves to a program for the refashioning of the domestic economy as well as the regulation of the international.

The acceptance of this program by many of the pacifists reflects the idealistic and radical nature of their thought. Many Protestant ministers, for example, looked forward toward a democratic socialist state. Their socialism was not often a doctrinaire Marxist variety, but a socialism which had its roots in the cooperative communal experiments of a century before, in the thought of Henry George, and, most significant of all, in the Church Christian Socialism of the social gospel movement. Its emphases were on ". . . gradualism rather than revolution, brotherhood in a classless society rather than class war."[79] It was the socialism that had been preached by W. D. P. Bliss, George Herron, and Walter Rauschenbusch.[80]

Tittle, for example, looked forward to a "cooperative common-

[77] Ernest Fremont Tittle, "Preaching and Practicing Peace," *The Christian Century,* LII (April 3, 1935), 443.

[78] Norman Thomas, "War, Politics, and Economics," *The World Tomorrow,* V (January, 1922), 12.

[79] Gabriel, *American Democratic Thought,* p. 318.

[80] *Ibid.,* pp. 315-330.

wealth;[81] Allan Hunter challenged the pacifists to devote themselves to the building of the classless society.[82] H. Richard Niebuhr called for a divorce from capitalism;[83] and Albert Palmer desired a "brotherly" social and economic order.[84] Norman Thomas, the tireless standard bearer for the Socialists, defined the ultimate struggle as that between socialism and capitalism, rather than that between democracy and fascism.[85] One student pacifist expressed succinctly the socialist's understanding of the cause of war: ". . . as long as the conduct of industry is concentrated in the hands of men who are responsible chiefly to those who have invested their money but not to those who have invested their lives in the products, there will be wars. . . ."[86]

There were even a few revolutionary socialists in the pacifist ranks, despite the seeming incongruity. They were Marxists who accepted the inevitability of the class struggle but sought to substitute a non-violent method of achieving the proletarian victory. They preached capitalism as the breeder of wars and imposed their class terminology on international and domestic events. Reinhold Niebuhr in the early thirties before he gave up his pacifism called himself a Christian Marxist.[87] The outspoken leader of this element of pacifist thought was Harry F. Ward, who like Niebuhr and Fosdick was a professor at Union Theological Seminary. This understanding of the nature of war is nowhere better characterized than in A. J. Muste's description of the American Revolution:

> . . . the American cotton growers and merchants who united to fight the war for independence from England and persuaded the masses of farmers and city artisans that it was a war for the principles of the Declaration of Independence, used their victory to establish a slave regime in the south and in the north a capitalism that has not differed much from the British model. It is certainly a debatable question whether over a century and two-thirds ordinary people in America or anywhere else have been any better off than if the Revolutionary war had not been fought or had resulted differently.[88]

[81] Ernest Fremont Tittle, "Preaching and Practicing Peace," *The Christian Century,* LII (April 3, 1935), 443.

[82] Allan Armstrong Hunter, "Pacifists and the United Front," *The Christian Century,* LIII (January 8, 1936), 49.

[83] Helmut Richard Niebuhr, "The Grace of Doing Nothing," *The Christian Century,* XLIX (March 23, 1932), 379.

[84] Albert W. Palmer, "If America Is Drawn into War, Can You, As a Christian, Participate in It, or Support It?" *The Christian Century,* LVIII (January 8, 1941), 53.

[85] Norman Thomas, "War, Politics, and Economics," *The World Tomorrow,* V (January, 1922), 67.

[86] Dorothea de Schweinitz, "Peacewards with the Younger Generation," *The World Tomorrow,* V (January, 1922), 23.

[87] Reinhold Niebuhr, "Why I Leave the F. O. R.," *The Christian Century,* LI (January 3, 1934), 19.

[88] A. J. Muste to the Editor of *The Christian Century, The Christian Century,* LVII (September 11, 1940), 1117.

The revolutionary pacifists saw in the advent of Hitler the twilight of capitalism; their task was the overwhelming one of stemming the flood of violence which threatened to accompany the ushering in of the new day of the proletarian utopia.

Thus, far from being innocent of the so-called economic causes of war, the weight of pacifist thought sided with the socialist and Marxist criticisms of the national and international economic structure. In fact, it can be said that the very vigor of their economic thought removed them from the main stream of American life into diverse channels of radicalism. The charge of radicalism added to that of utopianism removed the possibility of wide-spread public support for their crusade against war.

The pacifists accepted as a corollary to the theory that economic imperialism is the cause of war the proposition that aggression was no longer a meaningful concept in assigning war guilt. In fact the pacifist despaired of being able to assign any judgment on war guilt because the international economic structure was so intricate as to defy any attempt to determine the responsibility for provoking an armed attack. The revisionist historical writing was important in establishing this idea which had healthy effects in challenging uncritical patriotism and in introducing an awareness of the complexity of international affairs. But as a reaction to the facile designation of Germany and Austria as the villains of the First World War, the idea was carried to its other extreme which resulted in a suspension of all judgment.

In practice the idea did not result in a complete suspension of judgment. It took another form of redressing the balance by denouncing the acts of the Allies of the World War and excusing the aggressions of the defeated or "have-not" powers as a product of the greed of the victors. No single idea found its way into pacifist thought as often as did this. Villard in 1937 interpreted the First World War as a struggle in which England used Belgium as an excuse to knock out the German navy, the symbol of her most dangerous economic competitor.[89] He pointed out that the democracies had often been aggressors in the past, and concluded that there was nothing to choose between the Central Powers and the Allies.

When this sort of reasoning was applied to the current political situation in Europe it had deadly consequences, for it excused the actions of Germany, Italy, and Japan on the grounds that the democracies had not been perfect in their motivations; it established as a standard an absolute that had never existed. Hitler became the logical consequence of Versailles, or as Harold Bosley put it in 1938: ". . . the final agonized answer of an outraged people to those who seemed bent on

[89] Oswald Garrison Villard, "Another Word on Neutrality," *The Nation*, CXLIV (May 1, 1937), 508.

showing them no mercy."[90] John Haynes Holmes saw the appearance of Lloyd George and the Kaiser all over again.[91] Roland Bainton explained the dictatorship in Italy as a result of the failure to treat Italy as an equal at Versailles.[92] Georgia Harkness understood Japan's movements in the Far East as the "latest edition of Western imperialism."[93] H. Richard Niebuhr on the occasion of Japan's attack on Manchuria called for ". . . the inaction of those who do not judge their neighbors because they cannot fool themselves into a sense of superior righteousness."[94] Albert Day, to add still another example, pointed out that if we fought Japan we would be defending trade routes and supplies of raw materials that Japan required to satisfy human needs.[95] The reaction to this was to lump together all the nations of Europe as a contagion to be avoided by the United States. Donovan Smucker spoke of ". . . red, brown, black, and British imperialists. . . ."[96] Kirby Page labeled the European powers as "fascist Italy," "imperialist Britain," "militarist France," and "Hitlerite Germany."[97] British colonialism was equated by one pacifist with totalitarian dictatorship in Germany.[98] Villard capped this notion with his righteous indignation: "This is Christianity and humanity in March, 1939. And we are asked to defend with the lives of our sons two such monstrously unjust and stupid governments as those of France and England."[99] He was equally appalled, to be sure, by the cruelty of Hitler; the only alternative left for him and his fellows was an uncomfortable isolationism.

Not all pacifists were caught in the morass of disillusionment. D. Elton Trueblood, a Quaker spokesman whose pacifism had deeper historical and spiritual roots than the traumatic experience of the First

[90] Harold Bosley, "A Defense of Radical Peace Sentiment," *The Christian Century,* LV (November 2, 1938), 1324.

[91] John Haynes Holmes, "If America Is Drawn into War, Can You, As a Christian, Participate in It, or Support It?" *The Christian Century,* LVII (December 11, 1940), 1547.

[92] Roland Herbert Bainton, "Technology and Pacifism," *The Christian Century,* LV (May 18, 1938), 619.

[93] Georgia Elma Harkness, "What Can Christians Do?" *The Christian Century,* LVII (May 29, 1940), 700.

[94] Helmut Richard Niebuhr, "The Grace of Doing Nothing," *The Christian Century,* XLIX (March 23, 1932), 380.

[95] Albert Edward Day, "If America Is Drawn into War, Can You, As a Christian, Participate in It, or Support It?" *The Christian Century,* LVII (December 25, 1940), 1613.

[96] Donovan E. Smucker to the Editors of *The Nation, The Nation,* CXLIX (September 16, 1939), 303.

[97] Kirby Page, "If War Is Sin," *The Christian Century,* LII (January 9, 1935), 45.

[98] Harold Edward Fey to the Editor of *The Christian Century, The Christian Century,* LVI (June 14, 1939), 775.

[99] Oswald Garrison Villard, "Stage Set for Massacre," *The Nation,* CXLVIII (April 1, 1939), 378.

World War, described with a humility that set him apart from the other pacifist writers the dilemma the Friends faced once again in their opposition both to oppression and war. He recognized on one hand the "terrible menace and danger of Hitler" and on the other that his faith allowed him no choice but the way of peace. "There is no logical inconsistency," Trueblood stated, "in condemning what is patently evil and, at the same time, seeking to overcome this evil in other ways than the ways of military power. The Quaker tradition of active good will is as far removed from isolationism as it is from militarism."[100] But Trueblood's statement was a rare exception to the rule. No aspect of the pacifist doctrine of the First World War met with more bitter rebuke from certain quarters than its refusal to see in Hitler and his cohorts a challenge to the survival of Western civilization.

Many present-day political scientists and historians looking back at the two World Wars place primary stress on political factors as the primary causes of the war. Basic was a struggle for power; other factors usually ascribed as causes were secondary expressions of this primary drive arising out of the very nature of the nation-state system. In the writings of the pacifists this emphasis was conspicuously absent. The phrases "balance of power system" or "treaty alliance system" cropped up occasionally but they were hastily passed over. Villard late in 1939 began to refer to the European situation as a "power-politics game."[101] Benjamin Musser and Devere Allen spoke of the power problem and secret diplomacy as contributory factors in bringing on war,[102] but this was the extent of their political interpretation of war.

The expression of power politics in the form of nationalism also received scant regard. It is true that Kirby Page treated nationalism seriously but like other pacifists he did not consider nationalism so much as a profound force rooted deeply in the history or psychology of a people as an irrational set of slogans or doctrines to be discarded as soon as people became aware of their harm to the world community.[103] Pacifists usually equated nationalism with excesses of patriotism. Page defined the force of nationalism as expressed in four "doctrines": national interest, national sovereignty, national honor, and national patriotism.[104] To uphold these "doctrines" nations built armaments. Soon

[100] David Elton Trueblood, "The Quaker Way," *The Atlantic Monthly,* CLXVI (December, 1940), 744.

[101] Oswald Garrison Villard, "Issues and Men," *The Nation,* CXLIX (September 2, 1939), 247.

[102] Benjamin Francis Musser, "On Poetry and War," *The Catholic World,* CXXXIX (September, 1934), 706; Devere Allen, "Prerequisites of Peace," *The World Tomorrow,* V (November, 1922), 327.

[103] Kirby Page, "A New National Preparedness," *The Forum,* LXXXI (February, 1929), 70-74.

[104] *Ibid.,* 70-71.

a competitive race in arms developed which created the emotions of fear and suspicion which in turn resulted in war.[105] The pacifists saw the root of nationalism in the sin of greed; but they saw little else. It was irrational, unnatural; it could and should be cured. Nationalism thus was given relatively little notice and when it was seriously considered it was understood as an exaggerated expression of patriotism rather than as an historical force.

Militarism likewise was downgraded in the pacifists' hierarchy of causes. The armaments race was widely denounced and fought by pacifists who saw it as an immediate cause for the outbreak of war. The War Department received its share of imprecations also. Kirby Page described this facet, tracing its baneful psychological effects in producing a climate of fear and distrust and a confidence in the use of violence. Page was personally inclined to see in this process of military preparedness the primary cause of war.[106] Nevertheless, in their earnest attempt to be economic realists the pacifists understated the political cause of war in its expressions in the form of nationalism and militarism. It was on this aspect of their political unreality that Reinhold Niebuhr lowered the full weight of his criticism of the pacifists for he had come to see with the rise of the dictators the historical relativity of power politics.

Several pacifist writers attempted to understand war as a social and psychological phenomenon. Reinhold Niebuhr while still within the orbit of pacifism formulated the most ambitious explanation of the social origins of war. He assumed that there existed in society a normal state of equilibrium between the conditions of excessive fear and excessive trust. The concept of equilibrium he derived from his definition of human nature as ". . . an intriguing amalgam of potential virtue and inchoate vice, in proportions sufficiently variable to prompt both trust and fear."[107] The group, he said, was less bound by morality than the individual, which increased the dangers of exaggerated fear or trust. The exaggerated fear or "fear complex" might result from a shocking experience involving dishonesty or aggression. The excess of trust resulted from the concept that trust itself can create good, or peace, or reconciliation without any reference to the actual conditions causing distrust. A ready example (and probably the source of Niebuhr's argument) lay at hand in the Kellogg-Briand Pact which attempted to eliminate war by creating an atmosphere of trust rather than searching

[105] *Ibid.,* 71.

[106] Kirby Page, "The Menace of Military Preparedness," *The World Tomorrow,* IX (October, 1926), 163-165.

[107] Reinhold Niebuhr, "A Critique of Pacifism," *The Atlantic Monthly,* CXXXIX (May, 1927), 637.

out the injustice that leads to war. The excess of either fear or trust, then, produced an instability in society that made war an immediate likelihood.

The source of dishonesty or aggression which aroused the fear complex was found in the tendency of the group to be selfish. While men were concerned to some degree about their ethical relations to the group they were disposed to condone less ethical practices by the group as a whole and failed to see the implications of group action. In this group selfishness Niebuhr saw the root of war. Translating "group" into "nation" and "selfishness" into "power impulse" one discovers in this statement a picture of the political realities of the nation-state system. Written in 1927, the statement was prophetic in revealing Niebuhr's uneasiness with pacifism.[108]

Dwight C. Smith and George A. Coe emphasized the role of education as a contributing factor toward preparing the individual for participation in war. Both spoke of the role of the schools in producing a "mind-set" that would predispose the individual to accept war as the ultimate recourse of the state. Militarism in textbooks and uncritical patriotic exercises such as saluting and pledging allegiance to the flag were believed to induce the student to follow the call of the nation without reflection.[109]

Psychological explanations of war were confined to linking war to a primary human emotion such as fear or self-love, thus reducing the whole problem to a consideration of individual human nature and the function of education and ethical practice. E. Merrill Root proposed that war appears as an attractive alternative because the rest of life is dull. He did not suggest that this caused war but that it did make possible man's participation in it.[110] One practical psychological device received much attention. This was propaganda. Propaganda, considered not as a primary cause of war but as the trigger that discharged the passion and fear, as the artifice which overcame that "natural" tendency of men to peace and drew them into the army camps and onto the battlefields, as the clever manipulation of the love of country and freedom that made possible the sale of war bonds or the hatred of the enemy, posed a profound challenge to the pacifists. If it was true, as Villard claimed, that propaganda can sweep aside any resistance the people may have to going to war, how could he face about, as he did, and ad-

[108] *Ibid.*, 637-641.

[109] Dwight C. Smith, "How We Hate War!" *The Christian Century,* XLVII (November 5, 1930), 1338-1340; George Albert Coe, "Shifting the National Mind-Set," *The World Tomorrow,* VII (February, 1924), 42-43.

[110] E. Merrill Root, "Life's Bread and Wine," *The World Tomorrow,* IX (March, 1926), 71.

vocate trusting the reason of the people to decide such a weighty matter as a declaration of war through a national referendum?[111] There was a tendency in the pacifist thought of the inter-war period to grasp at any and all ideas that on the surface promised peace or created a fear of war despite basic inconsistencies.

In spite of the preponderant role played by theologians and preachers in the pacifist movement, a thorough exegesis of a spiritual or philosophical explanation of the cause of war was not worked out. The description of causal factors coming from the liberal Protestant differed little from that of the teacher or journalist. His thinking was secular, pragmatic, reflecting no deeper philosophy about war than that the evils or crimes of society have natural explanations and can be rationally perceived by man and that reason is capable of effecting a solution. His thought rested on the faith that man can construct on this earth with his own hands the Kingdom.

Ludwig Lewisohn was exceptional in offering a spiritual understanding of the cause of war.[112] He attempted to locate the cause of war in the history of Western civilization. He saw its root in the failure of European society to adjust to the Christian ethic it confessed. Lewisohn defined the Christian ethic as synonymous with the traditional Jewish ethic of justice, truth, and peace. These words were not cold abstractions but concepts emerging out of the daily life of a people. Justice was the means to create ". . . right, balance, and equity among men, to use mercy, and to abstain from the judging that destroys justice"; truth was ". . . all that has faithfulness and steadfastness. . . ."; peace was the spiritual health and welfare of the total man.[113] Lewisohn pleaded for an acceptance of life itself in all its richness, for living reasonably rather than dying bravely. The Christian ethic mixed with paganism had produced excess and morbidness. As Lewisohn put it, "Neither St. Francis kissing the sores of lepers nor the aged and satiated Tolstoy thundering against art and love can help us. Our duty toward lepers is to eliminate their disease; by art and love we live."[114] Mysticism, the knightly tradition of the Middle Ages, and the compromise with the rude inhumanity of paganism had betrayed mankind into the frightful irrationality of war. The regimentation of modern industrial society bred fear and a sense of insignificance that could be met, Lewisohn said, only with a return to the ethical humanism bound up in

[111] Oswald Garrison Villard, "Gentlemen May Cry Peace," *The Saturday Review of Literature,* XI (April 6, 1935), 606; Oswald Garrison Villard, "If This Be Treason," *The Nation,* CXLI (October 9, 1935), 399.

[112] Ludwig Lewisohn, "Levy versus Smith," *The Saturday Review of Literature,* V (March 9, 1929), 752-753.

[113] *Ibid.,* 752.

[114] *Ibid.,* 752.

the Jewish tradition of truth, justice, and peace. John Middleton Murray also spoke of war arising out of the spiritual barbarism of man in a technological civilization.[115]

The preoccupation of the pacifists with the subject of war made them sensitive to the currents in world affairs. Perhaps they were unduly impressionable, but beginning early in the twenties they saw the drift toward another disaster in which they saw the doom of civilization. In 1922 W. E. Orchard wrote, "It is quite conceivable that within the next twenty-five years new groupings, together with progress in militarism, might involve the whole world in a fearful struggle between the East and the West. . . ."[116] Two years later in 1924, John Nevin Sayre perceived that events were ". . . ominously drifting in the direction of a war which will break all records of frightfulness."[117] In the wake of the depression Reinhold Niebuhr and Harry F. Ward saw the awaited revolution draw near; ". . . an irreconcilable antagonism in the nature of capitalistic society is coming to a head . . . the day of conflict draws near," Ward announced.[118] Kirby Page and Oswald Garrison Villard early saw that the gulf between American and Japanese interests in the Far East was widening to the point where diplomacy would no longer avail.[119] Villard wrote in 1935: ". . . if the American people do not rouse themselves to the danger of our military and naval expansion, all of which is now aimed at Japan, we shall frighten Japan into an attack on us. . . ."[120] The only picture of the next war conceivable to the pacifists was that of the end of civilization, of famine, epidemics, chaos, and revolution.

Somehow despite the fright, the blood, the monotonous toil of 1914-1918, men went to war again in 1939. There was something about this that defied all comprehension. Never before had the peace message been more effectively brought to the world; never before had so many men of international and national fame and influence joined hands to preach peace. Villard wrote from London in September, 1939, his

[115] John Middleton Murray, "British Christians and the War," *The Christian Century,* LVIII (April 9, 1941), 491.

[116] W. E. Orchard, "The Basis for Internationalism," *The World Tomorrow,* V (November, 1922), 333.

[117] John Nevin Sayre, "War Is Unchristian, But - - -," *The World Tomorrow,* VII (February, 1924), 51.

[118] Reinhold Niebuhr, "Must We Do Nothing?" *The Christian Century,* XLIX (March 30, 1932), 416; Harry Frederick Ward, "Judgment Day for Pacifists," *The Christian Century,* LII (December 18, 1935), 1620-1621.

[119] Kirby Page, "Shall We Sign the Pacifist Pledge? Yes!" *The Christian Century,* LII (December 11, 1935), 1588; Oswald Garrison Villard, "Gentlemen May Cry Peace," *The Saturday Review of Literature,* XI (April 6, 1935), 606.

[120] Oswald Garrison Villard, "Gentlemen May Cry Peace," *The Saturday Review of Literature,* XI (April 6, 1935), 606.

poignant, pathetic verdict: "The unfortunate and discouraging thing about it all is that human beings will not learn."[121]

The pacifist ranks by 1939 had lost many of its notable captains; the tyranny of Hitler was an overpowering challenge. Albert Einstein, exiled from Germany in 1933, his home looted, his bank account seized, advised the Belgians to repair their defenses.[122] That same year Reinhold Niebuhr began to transfer his loyalty from pacifism to the militant defense of the Western democracies.[123] The Ethiopian and the Spanish wars forced Fenner Brockway and Sherwood Eddy to question the efficacy of pacifism in dealing with the power struggle.[124] Most Protestant pacifist ministers in the United States, nevertheless, seemed to have held firm. In 1939 a thousand of them reaffirmed their pacifist faith.[125] The outbreak of war that year saw Bertrand Russell and A. A. Milne in England step out of the ranks.[126] In 1941 Maude Royden announced that she too had been unable to sustain the faith. A pacifist during the First World War, a famous minister in London, Maude Royden had offered together with two other ministers to go to the Far East in 1932 and stand unarmed between the Japanese and Chinese forces to awaken the world to a renewed devotion to peace.[127] Her terse message to the American people in 1941 mirrored a grim determination: "Do not preach to us. Pray for us if you can. If you cannot, let us alone. We are doing what we can."[128]

Why had the pacifists failed to win the peace? Why had so many influential leaders, especially in the churches of the United States, failed to bring the millions of "peace-loving" Americans into the pacifist ranks? The taint of radicalism certainly prevented their message from receiving widespread acceptance. Their impracticality and utopianism set them apart. Only a dramatic demonstration of the power of pacifism could have awakened the vision of peace. The pacifist spokesmen formulated their doctrine of war on generalizations derived from the ex-

[121] Oswald Garrison Villard, "Issues and Men," *The Nation,* CXLIX (September 9, 1939), 272.

[122] *The Christian Century,* L (September 20, 1933), 1163.

[123] Reinhold Niebuhr, "Why I Leave the F.O.R.," *The Christian Century,* LI (January 3, 1934), 17-19.

[124] George M. Gibson, "The Flight of Moral Leadership," *The Christian Century,* LVIII (June 25, 1941), 829; Sherwood Eddy to the Editor of *The Christian Century, The Christian Century,* LII (December 11, 1935), 1594.

[125] "Christian Pacifists Take Their Stand," *The Christian Century,* LVI (March 15, 1939), 343; Harold Edward Fey to the Editor of *The Christian Century, The Christian Century,* LVI (June 14, 1939), 775.

[126] George M. Gibson, "The Flight of Moral Leadership," *The Christian Century,* LVIII (June 25, 1941), 829.

[127] *The Christian Century,* XLIX (March 23, 1932), 372.

[128] Maude Royden, "What Should a Briton Do?" *The Christian Century,* LVIII (April 16, 1941), 523.

periences of one war. It was a transitory, inadequate formulation. But most important of all, perhaps, was the fact that the pacifists lacked a distinctive message and mode of action in peace time and they refused to adopt a distinctive role in war time.

If one looks at the pacifist understanding of war, nothing is found that other men and other groups were not saying. They reflected the revisionism and disillusionment; they repeated the age-old maxims on war. Of more importance, they lacked a mode of action to capture the imagination of the people. There were no runaway slaves to aid. Everyone agreed with them that peace was desirable. The pacifist protest against the drift to war hardly rippled the surface of American life.

With the coming of war there was a path available for the pacifists to dramatize their devotion to peace. But they refused to take it. The pacifists might have courted prison sentences by breaking the law, by disrupting or sabotaging the war effort, by preaching pacifism to soldiers and civilians. Students of the abolition movement, for example, have shown that the shift in public attitude in the North from the violent hostility to the abolitionists in the 1830's to the widespread aid of fugitive slaves in the 1850's was the product, in part, of the examples of martyrdom in the abolitionist ranks. The desire for martyrdom or the recognition of the power of such a course of action was present in the writings of nearly all pacifists.

A few illustrations will reveal the turmoil and desire of the pacifist mind. Norman Thomas posed these questions in 1924: "Even if hundreds were without personal hatred but by steadfast refusal to cooperate, killed or imprisoned, do not thousands perish in war? And has not the blood of martyrs ever been more effective than that of soldiers?"[129] "Is it imaginable that, in this awful dilemma, we can escape reproach?" John Haynes Holmes asked, "[William Ellery] Channing did not think so, else he would not have spoken of the possibility of the pacifist's being 'hurried to prison' or 'brought thence to be shot,' nor added with a grimness unusual in so gentle a spirit, that 'there must be martyrs to peace as well as to other principles of religion.' "[130] Albert Palmer, writing in 1942 in the first months of the war, expressed the feeling that haunted the pacifist's spirit: "To every convinced Christian pacifist there must come at times a disturbing question as to whether, if he were a true successor to the prophets, apostles, and martyrs, he would not throw discretion to the winds and, cost what it might in persecution, imprisonment and loss of fellowship, to say nothing of wider reactions

[129] Norman Thomas, "Can Pacifism Act Against Injustice?" *The World Tomorrow,* VII (July, 1924), 211.

[130] John Haynes Holmes, "A Pacifist Minister to His Brethren," *The Christian Century,* LVI (November 8, 1939), 1375-1376.

in his family and friends, utter his moral and spiritual revulsion against war and his cry for peace."[131] This was the feeling of E. Stanley Jones when he said: "Just now I passed a sign in the window saying that the government wants blood for blood transfusions for wounded and sick soldiers. 'Ah,' I said to my companion, 'that I can do. If I cannot take blood, I can give it. In more ways than one I'd like to give it!' . . . for seriously, I should be willing to jump into the river, or its equivalent, to bring this war to a close, or shorten it even by an hour. For my vision of something else is undimmed."[132]

But there were no martyrs. The one distinctive action, that of refusing to serve in the armed forces, fell on the few pacifists of draft age. The humane program for these men set up by the government in the Second World War rendered this form of protest of no impact on a public engaged in war. The pacifist writers advocated cooperation with the government short of direct contribution to the war effort. None could escape giving support to the war in some way and in sharing its consequences whatever they might be. The pacifists chose to acquiesce. They deplored violence and conflict of any kind which this call to martyrdom involved.

If the pacifists showed themselves to act not unlike other men faced with the monstrous irrationality of war, they had devotedly maintained their protest during the sore trials of the inter-war period with the confidence that the truth they spoke would survive even another war. Their faith, for their protest was more a matter of faith and feeling than of thought, was set down in a few simple lines:

For borderline and nations are
Less than one life, one heart that sees
A brother linked as star to star
Souls born for immortalities,
No wrong is righted in the will,
In peace and war, of those who kill.[133]

[131] Albert Palmer, "What Should Pacifists Do Now?" *The Christian Century*, LIX (June 10, 1942), 753.

[132] Eli Stanley Jones, "What Should We Do Now?" *The Christian Century*, LVIII (December 31, 1941), 1636.

[133] Benjamin Francis Musser, "On Poetry and War," *The Catholic World*, CXXXIX (September, 1934), 705.

CHAPTER III

PACIFISM AND THE STRUGGLE FOR SOCIAL AND ECONOMIC JUSTICE

No event was more disconcerting to the faithful in the pacifist ranks than the news in the late months of 1933 that a serious rift had developed within the Fellowship of Reconciliation. American pacifism, long plagued by chaotic individualism and a lack of solidarity in thought and in organization, had looked increasingly to the Fellowship of Reconciliation as a source of strength and harmony, for it represented ". . . probably the most elect spirits of our entire ethical community."[1] There was a tragic irony in this fact, as *The Christian Century* pointed out, that a group devoted to the ideals of "fellowship" and "reconciliation" should find itself in the throes of a serious debate on its very purposes and ideals.[2]

Doubts and questions had troubled members for a long time, but the first open recognition of the difficulties occurred at the annual meeting of the Fellowship held at Swarthmore College, October 13-15, 1933.[3] Two questions received priority in the discussion. The first was the feeling on the part of members who had been with the group since its founding that it was letting go of its religious foundations. The Fellowship was, in origin, essentially an extension of the Quaker faith to those outside of its association. Edmund Chaffee, chairman of the Fellowship for 1933-1934, noted with deep concern a lack of interest in the worship activities of the organization; he sensed a desire to turn from the Christian orientation to some form of social idealism.[4] This situation, however, was eclipsed by a more immediate and, seemingly, more urgent, issue.

With the end of hostilities in 1918 the Fellowship had increasingly turned its attention to problems of economic and social injustice. This new direction in its interests raised the question of the relationship of pacifism to these situations. Officials of the Fellowship participated, for example, in the New Jersey textile mill strikes of 1926-1927.[5] This experience raised serious doubts as to the efficacy of non-violent resis-

[1] "A Regrettable Rupture," *The Christian Century,* LI (January 10, 1934), 46.
[2] *Ibid.,* 46.
[3] Edmund Bigelow Chaffee, "Pacifism at the Crossroads," *The Christian Century,* L (November 15, 1933), 1439.
[4] *Ibid.,* 1439.
[5] *Ibid.,* 1439.

tance in the battle against entrenched business interests. This participation was but one aspect of the acceptance by liberal pacifists of the doctrine that war has its roots in economic injustice, and, more specifically, in the capitalistic system. Thus to abolish war, it was first necessary to reconstruct the economic system within the nation and among the nations. The obvious point of departure, at least to the pacifist's way of thinking, was to associate with the labor movement, or the "class struggle," as they referred to it in the inter-war period. It was a heightening tension between the traditional peace ideal and the demand for economic justice that at last burst forth in the dissensions of 1933.

The Swarthmore meetings served only to reveal the wide divergence of thought, the impossibility of arriving at any consensus because the problem was interpreted from so many conflicting points of view. The meeting at last decided to poll the entire membership on the two fundamental questions: the maintenance of the religious orientation of the Fellowship and the relationship of pacifism to the class struggle.[6] A committee composed of Arthur Swift (chairman), Reinhold Niebuhr, Edmund Chaffee, and Charles Webber hastily prepared a questionnaire and distributed it to the 6,395 active members.[7] By the time the Council of the Fellowship met on December 6, 1933, 996 replies had been received, tabulated, and evaluated by Goodwin Watson, professor of psychology at Teachers College, Columbia University.[8]

The questionnaire is a fascinating document because it attempts to assess opinions and to provide for the possible shadings of each idea. The continuation of the religious emphasis of the Fellowship, the subject of the first question on the poll, was given an emphatic vote of confidence (758-187).[9] The second section of the questionnaire is intriguing because it illustrates the tenor of liberal pacifist thought on social and economic questions, and the perplexity of pacifists trying to apply their doctrines to specific problems. Members were to indicate which of six possible statements most closely approximated their conception of how far the Fellowship should go in identifying itself with the "class struggle." (The vote on each statement is indicated in parentheses.)

In seeking for a "social order which will suffer no individual or group to be exploited for the profit or pleasure of another" I believe the members and secretaries of the fellowship should go so far as to:

[6] *Ibid.,* 1440.

[7] Arthur L. Swift, "Fellowship Reverberations," *The World Tomorrow,* XVII (January 18, 1934), 40; Edmund Bigelow Chaffee, "Why I Stay in the F.O.R.," *The Christian Century,* LI (January 3, 1934), 16.

[8] Edmund Bigelow Chaffee, "Why I Stay in the F.O.R.," *The Christian Century,* LI (January 3, 1934), 16.

[9] *Ibid.,* 16.

(1) Proclaim the ideal of such a social order and endeavor through methods of love, moral suasion and education to bring in the new order, but refuse to identify themselves with either the underprivileged class or the privileged class to the virtual exclusion of the other. (210)

(2) Identify themselves with the just aims of the workers and underprivileged, and protest against the use of violence by the police, militia and underprivileged groups; raise and distribute relief to workers striking for a living wage; attempt peacefully to maintain the civil liberties of exploited groups and espouse publicly their aims, but without the use of any form of coercion. (191)

(3) Assist in organizing the workers into unions and in leading them in strikes for a living wage, and if need be in a non-violent general strike; assist in organizing the workers into a political party which will use non-violent political and economic coercive measures in order to secure the abolition of capitalism, but dissociating themselves from any group that used armed violence to gain its ends. (167)

(4) In case the legal owners of the essential industries resort to armed force in an attempt to maintain or to regain control of their property, refuse to use violence against them, but offer to serve the workers as a social worker among their families, as a maintainer of food supplies, as a nurse or stretcher bearer, or in other non-violent ways. (310)

(5) In the situation described in No. 4 consent to the use of armed force if necessary to secure the advantages of the workers, but regretfully and only while the necessity for it continues. (99)

(6) In anticipation of general class warfare, assist in the arming of workers and in other ways prepare them for the struggle; when war is fully joined, urge workers to acts of violence and participate with them in such acts. (19)[10]

The most striking feature of this questionnaire was not the fact that nearly ninety per cent of the membership reaffirmed a position of non-violence (Statements 1-4), but the radical implications of the commitment to the labor struggle. This questionnaire was designed to measure the degree of coercion to which Fellowship members would lend their aid; the result indicated that they would support the laboring classes in times of violence in noncombatant ways. Because the highest number of votes for any one position was given to Statement Four, the Council ruled that this position would constitute the bounds beyond which the Fellowship would not go.[11] This meant, however, that the Fellowship accepted all the activities mentioned in the first three statements as well; a rereading of these articles will bear out the assertion of the radical disposition of the pacifist thought of the period, for in-

[10] As quoted in John Coleman Bennett, "That Fellowship Questionnaire," *The World Tomorrow,* XVI (December 21, 1933), 690; Edmund Bigelow Chaffee, "Why I Stay in the F.O.R.," *The Christian Century,* LI (January 3, 1934), 15.

[11] Kirby Page, "The Future of the Fellowship," *The World Tomorrow,* XVII (January 4, 1934), 10.

cluded in the group of activities is the assistance to workers in the formation of a political party which will seek to secure the abolition of capitalism through ". . . nonviolent political and economic coercive measures. . . ."

The immediate consequences for the life of the society were the decisions that only "resolute" pacifists would be employed as secretaries, and that a special committee would be formed to secure new secretaries who were not hostile to the "Statement Four" position assumed by the group, but, at the same time, would not exceed it in their activities and sympathies.[12] By a vote of 18-12 the Council decided not to reappoint its executive secretary, J. B. Matthews, because he wished to go further in the acceptance of the necessity of violence than the Fellowship would endorse.[13] Francis Henson, Roger Baldwin, Bradford Young, and Reinhold Niebuhr resigned from the Council, believing the Fellowship should have allied itself uncompromisingly with the laboring classes.[14]

The questionnaire, while making somewhat clearer the general consensus of opinion, only served to intensify the debate on the problem of violence. To say that the membership divided into two camps would be a vast oversimplification, but the debaters did tend to be attracted to one of two poles. The majority in effect said that a member's position on the issue of the class struggle was a test of the sincerity of his pacifism in regard to international conflict. The minority tended to say that those who refused to subject all scruples about means to the demands of the hour—namely the supplanting of capitalist exploitation by a socialist state—were *ipso facto* defenders of the *status quo*.

This was the situation as Francis Henson described it in his "dialectical Marxist interpretation" of the events. He termed the action concerning the secretaries an "act of aggression" by the "right-wing" element. He characterized the meeting as ". . . the final blow to a working-class oriented fellowship."[15] Reinhold Niebuhr refused to go

[12] *Ibid.*, 10-11; Edmund Bigelow Chaffee, "Why I Stay in the F.O.R.," *The Christian Century*, LI (January 3, 1934), 16.

[13] Kirby Page, "The Future of the Fellowship," *The World Tomorrow*, XVII (January 4, 1934), 10; this is the same J. B. Matthews who in 1953 caused a furor over his charges that the rank and file of the Protestant clergy was filled with Communists and fellow-travelers, an accusation that cost him his new appointment as executive director for Senator McCarthy's Senate Permanent Investigating Committee. The interval between 1933 and 1953 had seen drastic changes in Matthews' loyalties. Paul Hutchinson, "The J. B. Matthews Story," *The Christian Century*, LXX (July 29, 1953), 864-866.

[14] Edmund Bigelow Chaffee, "Why I Stay in the F.O.R.," *The Christian Century*, LI (January 3, 1934), 16.

[15] Francis Henson, "A Dialectical Marxist Interpretation," *The World Tomorrow*, XVII (January 4, 1934), 8.

this far, for he could not denounce John Nevin Sayre, John Haynes Holmes, and Kirby Page as defenders of the *status quo*; yet he, too, had reached the place in his own thought where the distinction between violence and non-violence no longer had any relevance to the demands of the hour.[16] He described the failure of the Fellowship as a product of the prior failure of liberal Protestantism to recognize the coercive features of the economic and social order. It would be true, he feared, that pacifism ". . . will benefit entrenched interests more than it will help the proponents of a higher social justice when the day of crisis comes."[17]

J. B. Matthews hurled a ten point bill of particulars at the majority group in defense of his particular position. Most of these charges were concerned with details of the meetings, or interpretations of the questionnaire, but imbedded in his discussion were several assertions that challenged the fundamental assumptions of the Fellowship. He charged, for example, that there was a direct relationship between the amount of income a member possessed, and how he voted on the poll. Matthews claimed that of the forty most influential contributors to the Fellowship, thirty-six had voted for either Statement One or Statement Two on the questionnaires.[18] This sort of doctrinnaire economic determinism questioned the religious motivation of the group. Henson reiterated this view by contending that the same group which voted for the maintenance of the religious orientation, voted for the adherence to pacifism in the class struggle: "This signifies that for many today [like Henson] the only worthwhile religion is inextricably related to the struggle to build a new civilization."[19]

Matthews further challenged the logic of the Fellowship position. An established pacifist doctrine said that it was wrong for a minister to serve as a military chaplain because it meant moral entanglement with the waging of war. Now, Matthews asked, was not that the very position the members wished to take in relation to the class struggle—identification with the workers but in a noncombatant function.[20] Furthermore, he wished to know how many "well-intentioned" middle-class persons had identified themselves with the worker's cause. Matthews' next point struck at the efficacy of non-violent resistance; the reliance on love, he felt, was ". . . productive of a social situation in which a

[16] Reinhold Niebuhr, "Why I Leave the F.O.R.," *The Christian Century,* LI (January 3, 1934), 17-18.

[17] *Ibid.,* 18.

[18] J. B. Matthews, "An Open Letter to Kirby Page from J. B. Matthews," *The World Tomorrow,* XVII (January 18, 1934), 40.

[19] Francis Henson, "A Dialectical Marxist Interpretation," *The World Tomorrow,* XVII (January 4, 1934), 8.

[20] J. B. Matthews, "An Open Letter to Kirby Page from J. B. Matthews," *The World Tomorrow,* XVII (January 18, 1934), 41.

'warlike' revolution is made more certain."[21] The final proposition in Matthews' statement brought into the light an assumption often hidden in modern pacifism. "If personal detachment from violent acts exculpates you morally from the violence of those with whom you identify yourself," he asked, "do you not offer the same moral absolution to that overwhelming company of capitalists who personally commit no acts of overt violence. . . ?"[22]

The Henson-Matthews minority made their choice. The social ideal of the proletarian revolution was their goal; the means were to be pragmatically chosen, even violence if necessary, though it was to be avoided if at all possible. The majority, on the other hand, while claiming their devotion to the laborer's cause, limited in advance their method to that of nonviolence, declaring that this was a pragmatically valid choice as well, for only by non-violent means could the good society be established. But they often failed to recognize that their assurance about the pragmatic quality of non-violence came not from practical experience, but from their devotion to another ideal, the Kingdom of Peace on earth. To them the means used affected the ends; only the purity of the former would justify the endeavors for the latter.

The majority element advocating non-violence hastened to defend their radicalism. Arthur Swift pointed out that seventy-nine per cent on the questionnaire voted to identify themselves with the underprivileged.[23] Kirby Page reminded J. B. Matthews that in 1932 he had conducted a poll of the Fellowship membership on their voting preferences in the national election; the result was an overwhelming margin for Norman Thomas.[24] Page argued that the majority did not stop at mere love and moral suasion, but endorsed methods of economic and political coercion, which, in comparison to the traditional reliance on violence, were far more radical. The pacifists had not repudiated coercion, but sought to employ it more intelligently. Page felt that there was no difference in aim or goal between the factions.[25] John Bennett warned about the promiscuous use of the phrase "class war," which seemed to suggest that barricades were about to be thrown across the streets of New York or Detroit. He thought it doubtful if more than a minority of American workers would ever be class conscious: "To talk in terms of class war would be to consolidate the rest of the community—the farmers, the middle-classes, as well as the most privileged groups—in the name of law and order against the worker," not to mention the military power

[21] *Ibid.,* 41.

[22] *Ibid.,* 42.

[23] Arthur L. Swift, "Fellowship Reverberations," *The World Tomorrow,* XVII (January 18, 1934), 40.

[24] Kirby Page, "The Future of the Fellowship," *The World Tomorrow,* XVII (January 4, 1934), 10.

[25] *Ibid.,* 11.

of the state.[26] Edmund Chaffee reflected that to be called pro-capitalist had a strong resemblance to the experience of the First World War when pacifists were popularly denounced as pro-German. He saw in the results of the poll, as Page had, a vigorous assertion of the Fellowship's identification with the working class, the very antithesis of the so-called "swing to capitalism."[27]

A few voices of moderation were heard, but not heeded. *The Christian Century* warned that the Fellowship was constructing a creed for situations that were wholly hypothetical.[28] Elizabeth Gilman, a member of the Executive Committee, thought the whole business a species of "heresy hunting," though she revealed her sympathies when she pondered as to whether the differences of opinion had not arisen from the fear of some that the Fellowship was taking too strong a stand against capitalism.[29]

Three problems seem to present themselves from the consideration of this controversy: what were the sources of the radicalism common to all those participating in the debate; what were the nature and implications of the debate on the problem of violence or non-violence as the method of effecting social change; what specific aspects of social and economic injustice challenged pacifist thought?

The seedbed of modern pacifism was the social gospel movement. A brief look at this social and religious phenomenon will help to clarify the philosophy of the pacifists—what they envisioned, the terms they used, and the methods they chose. The social gospel movement embodied a complex pattern of ideas and attitudes. It meant different things to different men at different times, for it could not escape the determining hand of history. J. Neal Hughley has defined it as a climate of opinion characterized by ". . . a theological liberalism combined with a pronounced social idealism and utopianism—which prevailed in the Christian world in the United States at a particular time [1850-1920]."[30] Like most definitions, this admirably concise summary leaves unanswered a score of questions.

The historical roots of the social gospel were diverse. The contemporary industrialization and urbanization created a demand for a

[26] John Coleman Bennett, "That Fellowship Questionnaire," *The World Tomorrow,* XVI (December 21, 1933), 691.

[27] Edmund Bigelow Chaffee, "Why I Stay in the F.O.R.," *The World Tomorrow,* XVI (December 21, 1933), 691.

[28] "A Regrettable Rupture," *The Christian Century,* LI (January 10, 1934), 46.

[29] Elizabeth Gilman to the Editors of *The World Tomorrow, The World Tomorrow* XVI (December 21, 1933), 695.

[30] J. Neal Hughley, *Trends in Protestant Social Idealism* (Morningside Heights, New York: King's Crown Press, 1948), p. 2. (Hereinafter cited as Hughley, *Protestant Social Idealism.*)

religion adapted to the special needs of people living in the new conditions these forces produced. Umphrey Lee suggested that the reorientation of the church in terms of an increasing concern with social problems was partly the product of the soul-stirring impact of the anti-slavery movement upon Northern churches; ". . . a tremendous reservoir of moral enthusiasm remained unexhausted."[31] The philosophical preparation has been traced to the eighteenth century humanitarian ideal of the free and autonomous individual; the theological preparation must be largely attributed to Unitarianism with its optimistic faith in the nature and potentialities of man, its definition of salvation in terms of "character culture;" and its doctrine of the unity and immanence of God.[32] Undergirding and influencing all these forces was the expanding horizon of science. Darwinism especially made its impact felt on the religious life of the latter half of the nineteenth century. To the social gospel movement it contributed a solidaristic view of human society and reinforced the concept of an immanent God.[33]

The social gospel was, as its name implies, a socially oriented religion; it was anti-theological and anti-ecclesiastical in temperament, but it could not escape the task of refashioning theological terms to bring them into harmony with the new found social vision. The Fatherhood of God and the brotherhood of man have become as familiar as the phrases of the Declaration of Independence, as sacred as the Constitution. They implied a God of love rather than of judgment, and a unity of mankind—pregnant ideas for a nation emerging as a world power. Most distinctive of social gospel thought was the ideal of the Kingdom of God to be realized in history. Ralph Gabriel defined this Kingdom as ". . . expressed in co-operation rather than competition, in altruism rather than egoism, in human solidarity rather than strife. God is the bond which unites all men of whatever creed, nation, or race. Only by His aid can men hope for freedom, peace, and justice."[34] The Kingdom goal was not a collectivist state but ". . . a social order which will best guarantee to all personalities their freest and highest development."[35] In essence the Kingdom was to be the realization of the democratic ideal in all social relationships. Paralleling the assertion of the ideal of this earthly

[31] Umphrey Lee, *The Historic Church and Modern Pacifism* (New York: Abingdon-Cokesbury Press, 1943), p. 189. (Hereinafter cited as Lee, *Historic Church.*)

[32] Ralph Henry Gabriel, *The Course of American Democratic Thought: An Intellectual History Since 1815* (New York: The Ronald Press Company, 1940), p. 332. (Hereinafter cited as Gabriel, *American Democratic Thought.*); Charles Howard Hopkins, *The Rise of the Social Gospel in American Protestantism 1865-1915* (New Haven: Yale University Press, 1940), p. 4. (Hereinafter cited as Hopkins, *Social Gospel.*)

[33] Hopkins, *Social Gospel,* p. 123.

[34] Gabriel, *American Democratic Thought,* p. 329.

[35] Lee, *Historic Church,* p. 198.

Kingdom was the attempt of critical scholars to rediscover the historical Jesus. The Jesus they found was a social teacher who enjoined His followers to obey the law of love in all of life.

The main contribution of the social gospel to religious thought was the acceptance of the sociological concept of environmentalism.[36] Salvation thus became a social and ethical transformation of the individual, realized in an attitude of stewardship toward all of life. The character of the "socialized individual," sensitive to all human needs, rather than a revolution of the masses, was to be the instrument for creating the just social order. The social gospel movement, however, moved beyond the idea of stewardship to that of Christian Socialism. Throughout the life of the movement distinguished leaders embraced the socialist faith. Reverend Jesse Jones, a Congregational minister of North Abington, Massachusetts and a pioneer in calling for a socialized religion, adopted socialism and founded the Christian Labor Union.[37] William Dwight Porter Bliss, with his Christian Association for the Advancement of the Interests or Labor, George Herron, and Walter Rauschenbusch followed in his footsteps.[38] Christian Socialism matured, not from the dialectical materialism of Marx or anarchistic socialism, but from a social idealism which stressed cooperation, brotherhood, and gradualism, and which sought its justification in non-material religious faith and values.[39]

The social gospel was also a religious expression of the progressive movement.[40] It was optimistic and democratic. Like progressivism, it was an evangelical faith, centering its attention upon the primary concerns of the progressives: the conditions of labor and the regulation of industry. The "institutional" church was the product of this desire to meet the social needs of an urbanized, industrialized community. The problems of war, imperialism, and racial discrimination were almost entirely ignored.[41] The absence of any discussion of pacifism in Hopkins' *The Rise of the Social Gospel in American Protestantism* would seem to indicate that the union of the social gospel and pacifism occurred during or after the First World War. The union, moreover, involved a reciprocal impact, for pacifism directed the various forms of religious social idealism toward a consideration of international problems and to an introspective analysis of the means for affecting social change.

Turning to the thought of the pacifists in the inter-war period,

[36] *Ibid.*, p. 185.
[37] Gabriel, *American Democratic Thought*, p. 306.
[38] *Ibid.*, pp. 316, 320; Hopkins, *Social Gospel*, p. 227.
[39] Hopkins, *Social Gospel*, p. 227.
[40] Gabriel, *American Democratic Thought*, p. 332.
[41] Lee, *Historic Church*, p. 204.

vivid illustrations present themselves of these elements of the social gospel. Georgia Harkness, describing the theological assumptions basic to modern pacifism, merely rephrased social gospel doctrines. She spoke of God as Father of all men, as dwelling within and beyond the course of history, and as dealing with men through "redemptive love;" of Christ as one known through the words and deeds of the historic Jesus found in the synoptic gospels; of man (here she made a concession to the criticism of liberal Protestantism by Niebuhr) as possessing the image of God within him, but an image marred by sin; and of the kingdom as ". . . the active responsibility for helping to create those conditions of economic justice, international cooperation and personal understanding through which God can progressively establish his Kingdom."[42] John Haynes Holmes envisioned the kingdom in like terms: ". . . a universal realm upon this earth which shall absorb all tribes and clans, principalities and powers, and make them one sovereignty of God . . . the incarnation in men's lives of the spirit of universal love."[43]

Like the social gospel thinkers and ministers, the pacifists tended to speak of "Jesus" rather than "Christ," and they actively identified Him with non-violent resistance. Allan Hunter repeatedly spoke of "The Carpenter of Nazareth" as a means of identifying Jesus with the laboring classes.[44] A striking example of this process of identification is found in the thought of Kirby Page:

> If Jesus were alive today and exhibited the attitudes and indulged in the practices which characterized his career in Palestine, he would certainly be regarded as a dangerous and subversive citizen. His name would appear prominently on numerous blacklists; he would run the risk of being tarred and feathered by Nordic Christians; he would be labeled a Bolshevik by reactionaries; he would be called yellow and treasonable by red-blooded Christian patrioteers . . . He sought to live every day as a good member of God's Home, and tested every attitude and deed by the criterion of the sacredness of personality, the principle of mutuality, and the practice of fellowship.[45]

A. J. Muste emphasized the "ethical teachings of Jesus;"[46] Albert Palmer based his refusal to go to war on the grounds that ". . . Jesus

[42] Georgia Harkness, "The Christian's Dilemma," *The Christian Century,* LVIII (August 6, 1941), 977-979.

[43] John Haynes Holmes, "A Pacifist Minister to His Brethren," *The Christian Century,* LVI (November 8, 1939), 1376.

[44] Allan Armstrong Hunter, "Pacifists and the United Front," *The Christian Century,* LIII (January 8, 1936), 47.

[45] Kirby Page, "Would Jesus Advocate Peace at Any Price?" *The World Tomorrow,* XII (January, 1929), 26-27; Kirby Page, "Is Coercion Compatible with Religion?" *The World Tomorrow,* XVI (March 1, 1933), 212.

[46] A. J. Muste, "Fight the Good Fight?" *The American Scholar,* VI (Summer, 1937), 334.

wouldn't do it . . .;"[47] and Paul Jones described love and sacrifice as the "methods of Jesus."[48] The spirit of the social gospel was vividly present in the thought of Harold Bosley describing the faith of pacifism as believing ". . . that the brotherhood of man and the love of God are not idealistic fictions but forms of ideal reality, seeking to inform and re-create the total life of man."[49]

A further reflection, both of the radical overtones of pacifist thought and the spiritual heritage of the social gospel, was found in the substantial wing of Socialists or Socialist "fellow-travelers" among the pacifists. Many pacifists gave ready assent to the statement: "War is an incidental denial of pacifism; Capitalism is the permanent denial."[50] They saw violence and class exploitation inherent in the profit-motive system. The socialism of the pacifists was idealistic and democratic in nature, yet Marxian terminology entered their vocabulary even though the dialectical materialism found few minds willing or able to commit themselves to its rigorous demands. Labor disturbances became the "class struggle," and the Kingdom ideal was now frequently proclaimed as the "classless society."

J. B. Matthews conducted a poll of 1,709 of the nearly 8,000 members of the Fellowship of Reconciliation on their voting preferences in the 1932 presidential election. Norman Thomas received the votes of 1,284 (75.1 percent), Hoover of 348 (20.4 percent), Roosevelt of 49 (2.9 percent), and Foster of 28 (1.6 percent).[51] Though Matthews was disconcerted by the surprisingly large vote for Hoover, the impressive fact of the poll was the clear expression of sympathy with the variety of socialism represented in Norman Thomas's Socialist Party. In Thomas himself was found the union of pacifism and socialism.

The World Tomorrow poll of the Protestant clergy in 1934 contained seven questions on economic problems. More than three-fourths of the ministers who replied endorsed such proposals as an inheri-

[47] Albert Wentworth Palmer, "If America Is Drawn into War, Can You, As a Christian, Participate in It or Support It?" *The Christian Century,* LVIII (January 8, 1941), 51.

[48] Paul Jones, "The Meaning of Pacifism," *The World Tomorrow,* XI (April, 1928), 164.

[49] Harold Bosley, "Illusions of the Disillusioned," *The Christian Century,* LVIII (January 1, 1941), 16.

[50] A. Fenner Brockway, "British Pacifists and the Revolution," *The World Tomorrow,* XV (November 9, 1932), 443. The distinctive conjunction of pacifism and Marxism in the inter-war period is noted and analyzed by David A. Martin, *Pacifism: An Historical and Sociological Study* (New York: Schocken Books, 1966), pp. 157-162.

[51] J. B. Matthews, "Pacifists Prefer Thomas," *The World Tomorrow,* XV (October 26, 1932), 402. This poll indicates a considerable shift in political orientation among the Fellowship members when compared to Chase's study of the 1928 voting habits.

tance tax to impose a "drastic" limitation on the wealth that might be legally inherited, and a "drastic" limitation through an income tax or removal of exempt status of the amount of income that might be retained. Eighty-eight percent rejected the pre-1929 form of capitalism in favor of a "cooperative commonwealth." Being asked to define the political form this "cooperative commonwealth" should take, 10,291 indicated a "drastically reformed" capitalism would best define it, but 5,879, or more than one-fourth, indicated socialism as typified by the American Socialist Party.[52] Among the pacifists who chose the latter definition were E. Stanley Jones, Reinhold Niebuhr, Sherwood Eddy, John Haynes Holmes, Ernest Fremont Tittle, Bishop Paul Jones, Henry Crane, W. Russell Bowie, Halford Luccock, John Bennett, Edmund Chaffee, John Nevin Sayre, and Philip Bernstein.[53] Devere Allen suggested that the union of pacifism and socialism was a logical one, for the gradualistic philosophy of gaining political power was proving too slow in the American experience. To avoid the terror and destruction of revolution, the pacifist could offer the peaceful technique of nonviolent resistance.[54]

The mood of discontent with domestic conditions was further reflected in pacifist strictures against capitalism. Their denunciations of capitalism were more emphatic even than their acceptance of socialism. To the causes for pacifist radicalism already noted must be added the "doctrine of the First World War," for war came to be seen as the product of economic injustice. This oversimplified economic interpretation was sound doctrine to pacifists, who proceeded to make an analogy between international affairs and domestic economic conditions. If rivalry between capitalist powers produced war, they reasoned, there must be inherent violence in capitalism itself. Their suspicions were confirmed during the inter-war period by major outbreaks of labor violence in the United States. War thus became simply a magnified demonstration of the evil present in the domestic economic system. But domestic violence rarely appeared openly; the pacifists could only discern its effects: starvation, unemployment, the gross disparity in wealth. Always, however, there was the threat of violence present; behind the exploiters stood the police, the militia, and the army.

This note of the inherent violence in capitalism pervaded pacifist thought. John Bennett argued, ". . . capitalism is based upon coercion and violence . . . it is destructive of human life and human values on a colossal scale . . . a ruthless system which results in starvation, disease,

[52] Kirby Page, "20,870 Clergymen on War and Economic Injustice," *The World Tomorrow,* XVII (May 10, 1934), 227.

[53] *Ibid.,* 235.

[54] Devere Allen, "Pacifism in the World Crisis," *The World Tomorrow,* XIV (December, 1931), 393-394.

death, warped bodies and souls for millions. . . ."[55] Sherwood Eddy called capitalism "Moloch-like;"[56] A. J. Muste, J. B. Matthews, and Roger Baldwin agreed that violence was inherent in the system.[57] E. Roy Calvert lashed out not only at the injustice of the profit motive and the private ownership of the means of production and distribution, but at the class lines capitalism produced; capitalism was a ". . . social order based upon personal profits, rather than the common good; industrial employment so monotonous that by contrast war may seem an escape into adventurous living; and industrial control which appeals to force; the classes estranged from each other. . . ."[58] Roger Baldwin found that it was a system of "inequality and privilege;"[59] Fenner Brockway, speaking out of his experience in Great Britain, voiced this same feeling that capitalism destroyed the spirit of life: ". . . it is crushing the mind and imprisoning the spirit of millions; it is beating down the workers and peasants of the world to hunger conditions in order to maintain the profits and power of the possessing class."[60] John Haynes Holmes spoke of "economic autocracy;"[61] Devere Allen warned of "minority business rule."[62] Harry Ward, perceiving ". . . an irreconcilable antagonism in the nature of capitalist society . . ." declared that it was contrary to the principles of the Gospel.[63] As in their judgment on war, so in regard to capitalism, these idealists wished to see the means as ideal as the ends were noble. The evidences of injustice, inequality, or violence in the American economy called for complete rejection of the system because these manifestations testified to the impurity of the means.

A psychological consequence of this type of thinking was the ten-

[55] John Coleman Bennett, "That Fellowship Questionnaire," *The World Tomorrow,* XVI (December 21, 1933), 690.

[56] Sherwood Eddy, "Must We Face the War Problem Again?" *The Christian Century,* LV (November 9, 1938), 1365.

[57] A. J. Muste, "Pacifism and Class War," *The World Tomorrow,* XI (September, 1928), 365; J. B. Matthews, "Pacifists Prefer Thomas," *The World Tomorrow,* XV (October 26, 1932), 402; Roger Nash Baldwin, "Inside or Outside? Two Views on the Relations of Pacifists to Revolutionary Movements. II. Working Outside," *The World Tomorrow,* VII (July, 1924), 202-203.

[58] E. Roy Calvert, "Capital Punishment and World Peace," *The World Tomorrow,* XII (April, 1929), 158.

[59] Roger Nash Baldwin, "The Pacifist Attitude to Crime," *The World Tomorrow,* XI (June, 1928), 266.

[60] A. Fenner Brockway, "British Pacifists and the Revolution," *The World Tomorrow,* XV (November 9, 1932), 443.

[61] John Haynes Holmes, "Is Revolution an Issue for Americans?" *The World Tomorrow,* VII (July, 1924), 199.

[62] Devere Allen, "Pacifism in the World Crisis," *The World Tomorrow,* XIV (December, 1931), 392.

[63] Harry Frederick Ward, "Judgment Day for Pacifists," *The Christian Century,* LII (December 18, 1935), 1620.

dency to exaggerate the extent of labor unrest and economic injustice during the twenties and thirties. Violent labor strikes, the partial relapse of the trade union movement during the twenties, and—the most soul-searching event of all—the Great Depression gave ample occasions for gloomy meditations. Holmes announced that the ". . . class struggle has been joined on a hundred fronts, and is breaking out constantly into open warfare."[64] These events and foreboding prophecies must be credited with part of the responsibility for moving pacifist thought leftward; perhaps the depression more than any other experience accelerated this tendency. And so the pacifists employed phrases such as "class struggle," "class-war," "proletariat," and "class consciousness," despite their non-Marxian outlook, and without testing the relevance of these terms to the contemporary American experience.

Class consciousness became more than a descriptive term; it was elevated to an ideal, a test for those who were sincere in their social service. It was the necessary prerequisite for the successful establishment of the new social order. John Bennett defined it as a ". . . loyalty of the workers themselves as a class, including both the fortunate skilled workers and the underprivileged workers, to the cause of their own emancipation."[65] Bennett went on to explain that this did not violate the Christian concept of love, nor did it mean that the working class would become narrow and selfish in its outlook. On the contrary, it was a step to a higher ethical level because it demanded a great loyalty.[66] Bennett saw two areas demanding immediate action: the weakness of labor unions and their failure to organize in large areas of the country, and the problem of the periodic depression of which the worker was a hopeless victim.[67] A. J. Muste declared that the identification with the class struggle was an imperative for anyone who desired to follow the teachings of Jesus.[68] Reinhold Niebuhr felt this imperative to accept the class struggle because education alone could never bring about justice.[69] The class revolution seemed to be the "wave of the future." Kirby Page uttered a solemn pronouncement that as the stage of industrialism advanced, class consciousness and "group solidarity" increased.[70] A few

[64] John Haynes Holmes to the Editor of *The Christian Century, The Christian Century,* LI (January 24, 1934), 112.

[65] John Coleman Bennett, "Christianity and Class Consciousness," *The World Tomorrow,* XV (February, 1932), 47.

[66] *Ibid.,* 47.

[67] *Ibid.,* 48-49.

[68] A. J. Muste, "Return to Pacifism," *The Christian Century,* LIII (December 2, 1936), 1603.

[69] Reinhold Niebuhr, "Is Peace or Justice the Goal?" *The World Tomorrow,* XV (September 21, 1932), 275.

[70] Kirby Page, "But Evil Must Be Conquered," *The World Tomorrow,* IX (October, 1926), 168.

like Roger Baldwin and Harry Ward carried this one step further and proclaimed the inevitability of the class war. Class consciousness was to be only a temporary expediency, for the real objective was the end to all classes. Labor became thus the one agency which seemed to offer some hope of achieving the good social order; the established institutions had tried and failed in their missions.

The "classless society" was a conceptualization of the ultimate goal of pacifist endeavor. John Bennett, Allan Hunter, and George Coe interchanged this term with the Kingdom of God.[71] The prevalent mode of envisioning the utopia ahead was in industrial and economic phraseology. J. B. Matthews spoke of a ". . . commonwealth of socialist nations which have organized their economic life around the principle of production for use instead of for profit."[72] Allan Hunter called men to the task of so exploiting machines that men would not be exploited.[73] Anna Rochester had the same image in mind when she demanded a "socialized industrial order."[74] Cooperation was another favorite term used to express the distinguishing characteristics of the just social and economic order. Paul Jones expressed the sentiments of men like Page, Tittle, and Palmer when he said, ". . . the cooperative element is a primary one, standing ground for the idea that human life must be organized around a principle of strife will be completely removed, and it will be seen that the pacifist is upon a solid foundation in insisting that life must be organized around the cooperative principle if it is to survive."[75] Yet the pacifist never lost sight of the individual; unless personality was transformed in this process it would be a worthless endeavor—"There can be only one real aim in life, and that is to raise man to the stature of his own spirit."[76]

These, in brief, are what seem to have been the principal strands in the making of the radical idealism of the pacifist, and of his intense desire to associate himself with the underprivileged: the social gospel

[71] John Coleman Bennett, "Christianity and Class Consciousness," *The World Tomorrow,* XV (February, 1932), 49; Allan Armstrong Hunter, "Pacifists and the United Front," *The Christian Century,* LIII (January 8, 1936), 49; George Albert Coe, "When Pacifism Turns Sectarian," *The Christian Century,* LIII (April 3, 1935), 430.

[72] J. B. Matthews, "Pacifists Prefer Thomas," *The World Tomorrow,* XV (October 26, 1932), 402.

[73] Allan Armstrong Hunter, "Pacifists and the 'United Front'," *The Christian Century,* LIII (January 8, 1936), 49.

[74] Anna Rochester, "The Pacifist's 'Preparedness.' How We Can Work for Non-violent Revolutionary Change?" *The World Tomorrow,* VII (July, 1924), 213.

[75] Paul Jones, "The Meaning of Pacifism," *The World Tomorrow,* XI (April, 1928), 163.

[76] John Haynes Holmes, "Can We Still Be Pacifists?" *The World Tomorrow,* XVII (February 15, 1934), 87.

movement and the Christian Socialism which matured within its bounds; the experience of the First World War and the resulting conception of war and violence as a product of economic injustice; and the disillusionment of the inter-war period punctuated with violent labor unrest and the depression. One further reason, Harold Rotzel points out, may have accounted for this development. War is a negative concept and lacks the impulse necessary to sustain the pacifist testimony in times of peace. A maturing pacifism therefore sought a positive message and field of action, and found in labor, or thought it had found, at least, the agency by which the peaceful reconstruction of the world would take place.[77]

The debate on the question of non-violent resistance as a means of effecting social change proved inconclusive. Statements on both sides reflected the warring tension between conflicting social ideals more than it did cogent arguments on the efficacy of non-violent resistance as a method. The argument advanced by the defenders of non-violent resistance was essentially a negative one, which by showing the failure and disaster involved in the use of violence, thereby secured the victory for non-violence by default. There was an either/or quality about these assertions strongly resembling the articles of the pacifist's declaration against war.

John Bennett and Devere Allen presented the fullest development of this type of thinking. Bennett, writing in 1933, declared that there was no real choice involved; non-violent coercion was a necessity as well as a possibility, for violence was unsuited to the times and to the American experience. He doubted, first of all, if there would ever be more than a minority of American workers who would be class conscious. To even speak in these terms, or to discuss such a thing as "class-war" would set the whole community against the worker; the military power of the state could crush an incipient revolt in a moment. But violence, furthermore, was self-defeating because once unleashed in the complexity of a modern industrial world, there would be no way of controlling or halting its course or directing it to the fulfillment of the social goals desired. Violence was self-defeating because society could never escape its hold if it was used as the means to a social revolution. The new social order created by violence would have to be maintained by violence.

Bennett did not develop the reasoning behind his statements, but it reflected the desire for pure means and the assumption that anything less would corrupt and defeat the ends sought after. He concluded by simply asserting that the possibilities for achieving social progress by means of persuasion and non-violent coercion had not yet been exhausted

[77] Harold Rotzel, "Pacifism in the Labor Field," *The World Tomorrow,* IX (March, 1926), 81.

in the United States.[78] Bennett, thus, saw only two alternatives; by proving or attempting to prove the inadequacies of the one alternative, he hoped to win adherence to the other.

Devere Allen, writing in the same year, developed a similar argument though it differed in detail; for him, as well, the terror and destruction of violent revolution were too great a price to pay for a new social order. Allen believed that violence reaped a harvest of vengeance and reprisals—a good example of the type of statements the pacifists were prone to make without subjecting them to historical criticism, e.g., in relation to the American Revolution. He added that unless a revolution were immediately successful, it would in fact hinder further social progress by delaying its realization for years; a defeated revolution was worse than none at all. Moreover, Allen said, the day of revolution had passed for an industrial nation like the United States; the idea of street barricades and home-made bombs belonged to past ages. It would be best to rid the mind of this kind of myth, for violent revolution was the "acme of impracticality." Allen concluded by pointing out, with real perception, the psychological effects of being committed to a program of violent revolution when the opportunity for such action never was present.[79] He called attention to the ". . . degree to which its advocacy serves as an anodyne for failure and as a substitute for effective action along other lines."[80]

Allan Hunter, repeating the dictum that violence was neither necessary, redemptive, nor historically probable, frankly admitted that the deciding influence in his thought was the desire for pure means. He would cooperate with labor in the achievement of its ends, but never would he violate his ideal of love and good will as the only ethical path available to him.[81] Jessie Wallace Hughan contributed to the debate by giving non-violent coercion a Marxian justification. According to Marx, she claimed, revolution, in the sense of a complete transfer of power, was to be brought about by economic power, not by war.[82] This argument was a further negative effort to validate the pacifist's dream.

John Haynes Holmes was more encouraging and positive in his defense of the pacifist technique. Centering his attention on the experience of Gandhi, Holmes was confident that the United States offered

[78] John Coleman Bennett, "That Fellowship Questionnaire," *The World Tomorrow,* XVI (December 21, 1933), 691-692.

[79] Devere Allen, "The False Lure of Class War," *The World Tomorrow,* XVI (March 29, 1933), 302-303.

[80] *Ibid.,* 303.

[81] Allan Armstrong Hunter, "Pacifists and the 'United Front'," *The Christian Century,* LIII (January 8, 1936), 49.

[82] Jesse Wallace Hughan, "Pacifists Face the Dilemma," *The Nation,* CXLV (July 17, 1937), 82.

even brighter hope for the success of the Gandhi method than India, for the United States had ". . . the inestimable advantage of an educated people, equipped with instrumentalities of democracy, trained in the exercise of self-rule, rich in the traditions of culture and liberty, and not yet overwhelmed by the crisis of instant action."[83] Holmes seemed unaware that these very qualities might just as well make Gandhian techniques more difficult to practice in the United States than in India.

Norman Thomas, political and intellectual leader of socialism throughout the inter-war period, gave thoughtful consideration to this problem. Like Bennett and Allen, Thomas's predisposition was to denounce violence as illogical and unnecessary. Feeling that violent revolution was a hopelessly risky thing in modern society, he wrote, "The more complex our society is, the further we are from the soil, the more dependent upon the intricate cooperation of many different groups in many parts of the world, the more devastating will be any large scale violence. . . ."[84] Thomas distrusted methods of non-violent coercion as well though he accepted them as a necessary alternative; for him the ideal means were persuasion and the winning of political control via the ballot box.[85] Thomas, however, was much too sensitive to the tensions of his time to content himself with wishful thinking; his look at history provided him with no easy answers. He found assurance in the fact that the development of the labor movement in the United States and Great Britain through the course of centuries produced only a ". . . tithe of violence which marked a single day when all was quiet on the Western front."[86] The measure of constructive achievement in proportion to the violence used provided an overwhelming justification for the peaceful democratic methods of change. Chattel slavery, Thomas further noted, had been abolished throughout the world without violence except in the United States.[87] This hopeful picture was dimmed, however, by other historical considerations. There was the "Western tradition of violence," the "incurable disposition" to accept it as inevitable.[88] No ruling class had ever voluntarily resigned its privileges. Political action through constitutional procedures was enervated by the procrastination and compromise inherent in these procedures.[89]

[83] John Haynes Holmes, "Can We Still Be Pacifists?" *The World Tomorrow*, XVII (February 15, 1934), 87.

[84] Norman Thomas, "Is Peaceful Revolution Possible?" *The World Tomorrow*, XV (September 14, 1932), 252.

[85] Norman Thomas, "What About the Use of Violence?" *The World Tomorrow*, XV (April, 1932), 105.

[86] *Ibid.*, 105.

[87] *Ibid.*, 106.

[88] *Ibid.*, 105.

[89] Norman Thomas, "Is Peaceful Revolution Possible?" *The World Tomorrow*, XV (September 14, 1932), 251.

From his experience and thought, Thomas drew some qualifying considerations to be applied to the pacifist ideology. First, until a better method than violence was agreed upon and perfected in practice, the laboring classes must never relinquish the threat of possible violence in whatever action they choose. For them to declare that they were committed without reservation to pacifist means would make them helpless pawns in the hands of the privileged class. The second qualification was that the responsibility for violence in industrial situations rested, not on the worker, but on the privileged who, whether by stupidity, selfishness, apathy, or deliberate act, created the conditions in which violence arose.[90] In the face of all these considerations, Thomas vigorously upheld his pacifism and his belief in peaceful democratic methods of change, but his ultimate loyalty was to the social ideal of the labor movement. The Spanish Civil War provided the toughest sort of test imaginable for the American pacifists; an accurate forecast of their reactions was impossible. A Marxian revolutionary socialist, for example, stuck to her pacifism in this time of crisis.[91] Norman Thomas, on the other hand, called for moral support and the shipping of weapons of war to the Loyalists, though he believed the United States should stay out of the conflict. Fascism, he decided, was a greater evil than war, at least in this situation where the working classes were fighting for their lives and their newly won government.[92] Thomas made a pragmatic choice determined in the light of the ideal of the probable effects on human personality.

The tension between pacifism as an ideal goal and means of action, or as a pragmatic alternative to achieve a social ideal was best illustrated in the life of A. J. Muste. Abraham John Muste was a central figure in the radical labor and reform movements of the inter-war period. Born in the Netherlands in 1885, Muste came with his parents to the United States in 1891, and grew up in Grand Rapids, Michigan. He received his education in Dutch Reformed parochial schools and at Hope College, where he achieved a brilliant academic and athletic record. After a year of teaching Greek at a formidable institution known as the Northwestern Classical Academy in Orange City, Iowa, Muste entered New Brunswick Theological Seminary, graduating in 1909.

While serving a church on the East Side in New York City and studying on his own at Union Theological Seminary, Muste was subjected to the impact of the thought of social idealists and reformers,

[90] Norman Thomas, "What About the Use of Violence?" *The World Tomorrow,* XV (April, 1932), 105-106.

[91] Jesse Wallace Hughan, "Pacifists Face the Dilemma," *The Nation,* CXLV (July 17, 1937), 82.

[92] Norman Thomas, "The Pacifist's Dilemma," *The Nation,* CXLIV (January 16, 1937), 66-68.

and the experience of the struggle for life in the midst of poverty, vice, and disease. This was at the same time that Norman Thomas was receiving his baptism in social work as a minister in East Harlem. In 1915, Muste accepted a call to the Congregational Church in Newtonville, Massachusetts, where a year later he made public his acceptance of pacifism by participating in the founding of the Boston section of the Fellowship of Reconciliation. The same year he joined the Socialist Party and struck up a friendship with Scott Nearing. The unpopularity of holding pacifist views at a time when the nation was marching to battle caused him to resign his pastorate in 1917.

Muste next appeared in a much different setting. Together with three friends, he joined the strikers at the Lawrence, Massachusetts, textile mills in 1919, rendering material aid and giving what counsel he could offer. On the tenth day of the strike, Muste was made chairman of the strike executive committee; he proceeded to win a signal victory in what appeared to be a hopeless situation. The labor movement now commanded his entire energies as he became general secretary of the Amalgamated Textile Workers Union. In 1921, a novel experiment was attempted in the labor ranks which Muste was well-fitted to direct because of his academic training. The Brookwood Labor College, established with the enthusiastic support of John Dewey at Katonah, New York, as the first residential school for laboring men, found in Muste an inspiring and gifted director. Roundly denounced by the American Federation of Labor as being communistic and by the Communist Party as being reactionary, Muste struck a middle course in his leadership of the school.

Muste founded and served as chairman of the Conference of Progressive Labor Action, an organization of left-wing labor leaders formed in 1929 to fight autocracy and corruption within labor's ranks and to stimulate the unionization of the basic industries. He envisioned a great labor party of thirty million members which could achieve through political action the liberation of the working classes. Between 1929 and 1936 Muste moved steadily to the left in his thinking. By now his pacifism was purely pragmatic and subordinated to his revolutionary social theory; he had severed all ties with the church and had rejected the Christian view of the world. His life was anything but calm during these years; in 1933 he resigned from Brookwood and from the Conference for Progressive Labor Action because his attempts to carry on both activities had brought hard feelings and bitter words from both groups. Muste's activities in reform groups were numerous and influential. He was an officer or council member of the American Federation of Teachers, American Civil Liberties Union, Pioneer Youth of America, League for Industrial Democracy, Committee on Militarism in Education, War Resisters' League, Fellowship of Reconciliation, United States Congress

Against War, a consultative member of the Committee on Churches and Social Service of the Federal Council of Churches, and a contributing editor to *The World Tomorrow.*

The most interesting and stirring crisis in the life of A. J. Muste, however, was his return to pacifism as the primary social ideal of his life at the very time when most pacifists were beginning to question seriously their faith. Disillusioned while traveling through Europe in 1936 by the war he saw in the making and the weakness of the European labor forces in the face of the new challenge, Muste walked into a church while sightseeing in Paris, and, in a moment, the whole course of his thought and action were redirected. The mere sight of the church interior was of such deep emotional meaning at this time in his career that he returned to the United States committed to pacifism and to the Christian faith once again. He assumed the directorship of the Presbyterian Labor Temple in New York City left vacant by the death of Edmund Chaffee. In 1940, he became the executive secretary of the Fellowship of Reconciliation.[93] The career of A. J. Muste seems significant because it reveals that basically pacifist thought was rooted in the psychological, emotional, and religious thought of men. A discussion of pacifist thought only considers the surface of ideas and rationalizations beneath which flow deeper currents that mold and determine the direction of this thought. Muste defended the use of non-violent resistance to bring about social change, but he too added a qualification to those of Norman Thomas; resistance to evil, even if it must be by violent means, was a higher ethical value than cowardly submission and acquiescence.[94]

While Muste pursued a circular route that brought him back safely within the ranks, many pacifists grew critical of the faith, or, at least, of its application to the class struggle. In 1924 Ammon Hennacy, a revolutionary socialist, defended his most unusual position of working for a violent revolution while remaining a pacifist. Hennacy believed that only by violence and hatred could the capitalistic regime be overthrown. In this struggle he intended to serve as a non-combatant that he might teach pacifism when the struggle was over and before the power generated by the revolution would swallow up the fruits of the victory. Not until men were economically free could they accept pacifism; pacifism alone would be able to preserve the work of the revolution.

[93] Biographical data on A. J. Muste are drawn from "Who Is This A. J. Muste?" *The World Tomorrow,* XII (June, 1929), 250-254; *National Republic,* XXII (July-August, 1934), 33; A. J. Muste, "Return to Pacifism," *The Christian Century,* LIII (December 2, 1936), 1603-1606; A. J. Muste, "Fight the Good Fight?" *The American Scholar,* VI (Summer, 1937), 334-344; A. J. Muste, "The True International," *The Christian Century,* LVI (May 24, 1939), 667-669.

[94] A. J. Muste, "Pacifism and Class War," *The World Tomorrow,* XI (September, 1928), 366.

But only a pacifist who had aided the workers in the time of struggle would be listened to, and so Hennacy prepared himself for his unique dual role.[95]

Harry F. Ward, professor of Christian ethics at Union Theological Seminary, chairman of the American Civil Liberties Union and the American League for Peace and Freedom, and general secretary of the Methodist Federation of Social Service, challenged pacifists to clarify the social ideal for which they were striving. Ward, writing in terms of the Marxian dialectic, saw in Norman Thomas's qualification concerning violence as originating at the top rather than the bottom of the economic order an ". . . indisputable law of history . . ." and that violence from below is a "cumulative process" in reaction to the use of violence from above.[96] While defending the usefulness of non-violent resistance, he added another qualification to its practical realization in the class struggle: another "indisputable law" that the armed forces must be won to the side of change before it could succeed.[97] The pacifist's role in preventing the revolution from becoming violent would be to appear at all points of labor unrest, denounce and expose violence, demand justice, interpose himself between the conflicting forces, and support organizations fighting industrial violence.[98] Ward went a step further in his thinking and decided that violence was sound "social strategy" when the conditions were serious enough to warrant it. The success of the revolution was the crucial issue at stake.[99] The minute this step was taken and full commitment was made to the social goal, pacifism lost its whole meaning and was relegated to a position of strategy. Pacifism was of significance only so long as it embodied both a goal and a method.

The profound critic of pacifism was Reinhold Niebuhr. As a pastor in Detroit from 1915 to 1928, Niebuhr came in constant contact with workers of the Ford Motor Company, an experience which taught him ". . . the penetration of idealism by the corrupting element of self-interest; the inevitability of self-deception in the best intention; the underlying cruelty and brutality in every class culture,"[100] and which

[95] Ammon A. Hennacy, "Inside or Outside? Two Views on the Relation of Pacifists to Revolutionary Movements. I. Working Inside," *The World Tomorrow,* VII (July, 1924), 201-202.

[96] Harry Frederick Ward, "Judgment Day for Pacifists," *The Christian Century,* LII (December 18, 1935), 1621.

[97] *Ibid.,* 1621.

[98] *Ibid.,* 1621.

[99] *Ibid.,* 1622.

[100] D. R. Davies, *Reinhold Niebuhr: Prophet from America* (New York: The Macmillan Company, 1948), p. 16. (Hereinafter cited as Davies, *Niebuhr.*); biographical data on Niebuhr are drawn from Davies, *Niebuhr, passim; Who's Who in America: A Biographical Dictionary of Notable Living Men and Women of the United States* (Chicago: A. N. Marquis Company, 1954), XVIII, 1774.

made him a social radical, indeed a revolutionary. In 1928 Niebuhr became professor of applied Christianity at Union Theological Seminary in New York. From his pen during the course of the inter-war period, and continuing to today, came the most challenging books and articles of any serious thinker in the United States. At the same time that his radical thought on social problems inspired basic discussion in the area of social and political philosophy, his writings on ethics and religion changed the course of American theological thinking. For here is encountered the central paradox of Niebuhr's thought; as he moved to the left on political and social problems, he moved toward orthodoxy in his theology, concluding that orthodox theology provided the firmest base for radical social thought because it alone portrayed human nature and history in their true light.[101]

As a critic of the liberal cultural tradition of the Western world, and particularly of Protestant liberalism, Niebuhr attacked the very foundations of modern pacifist thought. The irony of the situation was that he came out of the pacifist ranks. During 1932-1933, he was chairman of the Fellowship of Reconciliation and an editor of *The World Tomorrow.* Like Muste, his trek away from pacifism was a slow one, but, unlike Muste, Niebuhr moved farther away at the precise time that Muste returned to the fold. Niebuhr's attack on pacifism, and especially on the use of non-violent resistance in the class struggle was two-edged and, like everything else about him, paradoxical. In the early thirties his thought was strongly marked by his Marxist interpretation of the social order; thus his attack on pacifism centered heavily on the failure or unwillingness of the pacifist to devote himself completely to the cause of the laboring classes. There was no valid ethical distinction that could be made between violence and non-violent resistance, he declared. The true ethical consideration was the degree of identification with the demand for social and economic justice. By the mid-thirties, with the rising menace of the fascist dictatorships, Niebuhr's thought lost its obvious Marxian overtones, though he always has remained dialectically oriented, and the attack on pacifism now came more from the other side of his thought—the theological. It struck telling blows at the shallowness of the pacifist's understanding of nature, human nature, history, and Christian faith.

Though Niebuhr claimed as late as 1934 that he remained a pacifist in that he would refuse to participate in an international conflict, he had laid the foundations for a rejection both of that position and the use of pacifism in the class struggle several years before the break came in the Fellowship of Reconciliation.[102] In 1931 he defined religious rad-

[101] Davies, *Niebuhr,* p. 34.

[102] Reinhold Niebuhr, "Why I Leave the F.O.R.," *The Christian Century,* LI (January 3, 1934), 18.

icalism as having its basis in the conception of human nature as possessing both the qualities of the sinner and of the child of God. Nothing is quite so important in understanding Niebuhr as his conception of human nature as a mixture of good and evil with a slight edge given to the latter propensity in the processes of history—a conception which has led Ralph Gabriel to compare him with John C. Calhoun.[103] Secular forms of radicalism contributed to the religious forms the awareness of the brutality and violence inherent in the social order without which religious radicalism would easily degenerate into sentimentality and a confident reliance on the power of education and ethical conscience to effect social change (as in the case of pacifism). Secular radicalism—meaning some form of revolutionary socialism—was itself inadequate, however, because it underestimated the presence of the ethical in history and in human nature and it made its own goal or achievements the supreme values in life. Thus it was incapable of self-criticism.[104]

From the root understanding of human nature, Niebuhr fashioned his concept that in all of life there was the seed of corruption and that the religious revolutionist, alone having an absolute ideal that was beyond the stream of history, could always remain self-critical and sensitive to the imperfections of his own actions. For Niebuhr love was the standard of perfection incapable of being realized in history; all historical situations and judgments were no more than relative.[105] The tragedy of the pacifist was that he tried to persuade society to adopt the way of love, which he as an individual was sometimes able closely to approximate, but of which society reflecting the mixed elements of human nature was forever incapable. Niebuhr wrote that justice, not love, was ". . . probably the highest ideal toward which human groups can aspire. And justice, with its goal of adjustment of right to right, inevitably involves the assertion of right against right and interest against interest until some kind of harmony is achieved."[106] Justice then was to be a relative matter, the product of a conflict of interests resolved in a temporary equilibrium.

Moving from these general concepts, Niebuhr believed that there did exist a social conflict between the privileged and the disinherited in every Western nation.[107] As early as 1928, he asserted that there was no intrinsic difference between violence and non-violence, though

[103] Gabriel, *American Democratic Thought,* p. 386.

[104] Reinhold Niebuhr, "Radicalism and Religion," *The World Tomorrow,* XIV (October, 1931), 324-327.

[105] Reinhold Niebuhr, "Why I Leave the F.O.R.," *The Christian Century,* LI (January 3, 1934), 18.

[106] Reinhold Niebuhr, "Must We Do Nothing?" *The Christian Century,* XLIX (March 30, 1932), 416.

[107] Reinhold Niebuhr, "Why I Leave the F.O.R.," *The Christian Century,* LI (January 3, 1934), 18.

he saw the danger of violence being uncontrollable and the hopeful possibility of the pacifist keeping the struggle from turning in that direction.[108] In 1932 he reiterated the inevitability of the class struggle. Emphasizing the inherent selfishness of both parties to the struggle, he felt that the best that pacifism could do would be to impose some check on the extent of the conflict.[109] By 1934, he felt that a conflict of power and violence was inevitable, that to try to maintain the personal purity of pacifism while supporting the effort of the workers was to ignore the ethical implications of the struggle. Moral absolutes did not apply to the relativities of the historical scene; the weight of justice in this struggle rested on the side of the workers. Thus the only choice was either to support them by whatever means possible, or to deny justice by tacitly or openly supporting the privileged.[110] In the midst of this struggle, Niebuhr was quick to caution that the triumph of the laboring classes, if it came, would not usher in the long-sought Kingdom, for the new society would be afflicted with the same elements of corruption and imperfection which had destroyed the privileged.[111] It was a relative matter, a judgment made in relation to the alternatives actually present in history, but always subject to the eternal judgment of absolute justice. The awareness of both these aspects—the relative and the eternal—at one and the same time was the distinctive force that made religious radicalism realistic and capable of redirecting its own development because its earthly goals were never transformed into absolutes.

As a Marxian, Niebuhr perceived the peril to Western civilization in the capitalism he saw disintegrating before his eyes; as a Christian, he saw the equally disastrous peril in the materialism of Communism. Both meant barbarism; the cause of the class movement must somehow move in the treacherous and uncertain ground between the two. With an awareness of these relativities and of the absolute demands of God which could not be fulfilled in history, the individual had to fight without hate and with forgiveness; Niebuhr wrote in 1934: "I am no longer willing to express Christian purpose in social life merely by insisting that the Christian must be non-violent in his social relations. I know very well that violence may lead to chaos, but I also know that non-violent injustice may lead to death."[112]

[108] Reinhold Niebuhr, "Pacifism and the Use of Force," *The World Tomorrow,* XI (May, 1928), 218-220.

[109] Reinhold Niebuhr, "Idealism and the Social Struggle," *The World Tomorrow,* XV (October 26, 1932), 395-397.

[110] Reinhold Niebuhr, "Why I Leave the F.O.R.," *The Christian Century,* LI (January 3, 1934), 18.

[111] Reinhold Niebuhr, "Idealists and the Social Struggle," *The World Tomorrow,* XV (October 26, 1932), 396.

[112] Reinhold Niebuhr to the Editor of *The Christian Century, The Christian Century,* LI (January 31, 1934), 155.

As the democracies of Europe struggled to prepare themselves to meet the threats of Germany and Italy in the mid-thirties, Niebuhr became an eloquent spokesman for their cause, pointing out, nevertheless, the weakness and imperfection of the liberalism which pervaded their thought, but indicating as well, especially to the pacifists, the highly perceptive distinction that, while Marxism and the derivative economic interpretation of history which appealed to the generation of the inter-war period defined all injustice as springing from capitalism and imperialism, actually they were only the sources of economic injustice.[113] In the late thirties the specter of political and social injustice represented in the figure of Hitler was the supreme challenge to Western civilization. Pacifism, which oversimplified the forces of history and tried to determine its course of action, not in relation to the alternatives present, but in relation to an absolute ideal that never could be realized in history, was irrelevant, helpless, and incapable of facing the months of terror and destruction that lay ahead. Niebuhr summarized his attitude toward the liberal Protestant faith:

> It has sought to make a success story out of the story of the Cross, and has admonished men to be resolute in sacrificing their lives and interests because in that way they would not have to sacrifice their lives and interests; for their goodness would shame their enemy into goodness so that he would cease to imperil them. They do not understand that the perfect love of Christ comes into the world, but that it does not maintain itself there; that the Cross therefore stands at the edge of history and not squarely in history; that it reveals what history ought to be but not what history is or can be; and that Christian faith has quite rightly seen in the Cross a revelation of the nature of the divine and eternal as well as of the ultimate historical possibility and impossibility.[114]

The great debate within the Fellowship of Reconciliation was not brought about by long-standing intellectual doubts and questionings alone. A direct challenge to pacifists interested in social reform had been given a few weeks previous to the Fellowship annual meeting—a challenge forcing each member to take a stand on this precise issue of violent and non-violent means. The American Communist Party, speaking indirectly through prominent figures such as Theodore Dreiser and Upton Sinclair and reflecting in its actions the shift in Comintern strategy from a position of hostility to one of cooperation with democratic forces in an effort to combat fascism, invited those interested to join in a United States Congress Against War and Fascism to be held September 29 to

[113] Reinhold Niebuhr, "Must Democracy Use Force? II. Peace and the Liberal Illusion," *The Nation,* CXLVIII (January 28, 1939), 119.

[114] Reinhold Niebuhr, "If America Is Drawn into War, Can You, As a Christian, Participate in It or Support It?" *The Christian Century,* LVII (December 18, 1940), 1574.

October 1, 1933, in New York.[115] The response to the Congress, led by Robert Morss Lovett, Harry Ward, Lincoln Steffens, and Roger Baldwin, was quite impressive, for representatives of ". . . hundreds of liberal, pacifist, veteran, radical labor, student, and A. F. of L. organizations . . ." were present; in all there were 2,616 delegates from 35 states.[116] The Fellowship of Reconciliation, War Resisters' League, and Women's International League for Peace and Freedom were present on this first occasion of cooperation between peace and pacifist organizations and the Communist Party.[117] Notable for its absence was the Socialist Party which could not forgive the past warfare on the part of the Communists or take much stock in the sudden change of face.

It was not without significance, it would seem, that the United States Congress Against War and Fascism chose as its first chairman J. B. Matthews, who within three months was removed from his post as executive secretary of the Fellowship of Reconciliation.[118] The debate over methods and goals and the resulting poll of the Fellowship thus had a practical foundation in the immediate question as to the proper role of the pacifist toward participation in the "united front" with the Communists. Matthews influenced a group of Fellowship members to follow him into the American League Against War and Fascism, the name given to the permanent organization formed at the meeting of the Congress.[119] Two years later in 1935, Harry F. Ward succeeded Matthews as chairman of the American League, a post he held until the group disbanded in 1940.[120] Through its affiliated members the American League represented nearly two million people.[121] It maintained an air of respectability throughout its brief history; the Cleveland convention in 1936, for example, was addressed by the Republican mayor of the city and by Major General Smedley Butler. The Bishop of the

[115] Devere Allen, "War and the 'United Front'," *The World Tomorrow,* XVI (October 12, 1933), 571; Dixon Wecter, *The Age of the Great Depression 1929-1941* (volume XIII, Arthur Meier Schlesinger and Dixon Ryan Fox, eds., *A History of American Life*) (New York: The Macmillan Company, 1948), p. 306. The strategy of the "Popular Front" is discussed in Irving Howe and Lewis Coser, *The American Communist Party: A Critical History* (New York: Frederick A. Praeger, paper edition, 1962), pp. 319-386. (Hereinafter cited as Howe and Coser, *Communist Party.*).

[116] Devere Allen, "War and the 'United Front'," *The World Tomorrow,* XVI (October 12, 1933), 571; Merle Curti, *Peace or War: The American Struggle 1636-1936* (New York: W. W. Norton and Company, 1936), p. 286; Howe and Coser, *Communist Party,* p. 349.

[117] *The Nation,* CXXXVII (October 11, 1933), 394.

[118] Paul Hutchinson, "The J. B. Matthews Story," *The Christian Century,* LXX (July 29, 1953), 864.

[119] *Ibid.,* 864; *The Nation,* CXXXVII (October 11, 1933), 394.

[120] Clara Studer, "Peace and Its Wily Preachers," *The Living Age,* CCCLVIII (August, 1940), 558.

[121] Curti, *Peace or War,* p. 273; Howe and Coser, *Communist Party,* p. 351.

Methodist Church and a leading Jewish rabbi were present sharing the platform with radicals like Harry Ward, Earl Browder, and Roger Baldwin.[122]

In pacifist circles the reaction was vigorous, reflecting not alone a defense of unsullied pacifism, but of socialist sympathies as well. There were a few outspoken defenders of the "united front." George Coe and Harry Ward issued calls for an end to "sectarian" pacifism and for a new "inclusive" pacifism, by which they meant that all opposed to imperialistic war and fascism as the products of the capitalistic system should unite on the basis of their common social goals irrespective of differences about the means to the goals. Ward termed it an "absolute necessity" because the period of the decline of capitalism was at hand and the dynamic character of the Communists had been revealed. The Communists were not wedded to terror, he assured the pacifists; they would be delighted if the next stage in human society could be brought about by peaceful methods. He tried to impress the hesitant with the sense or urgency: "The form of transition to the new order is being determined now. An effective alliance to resist immediate subversion of democratic rights by the capitalist forces and to operate the democratic process for imperative social changes is the only way by which we may hope to avoid dictatorship."[123]

Coe and Ward attempted to meet religious objections to the compromise by shaming the Christians. Coe commented that the Communists had foregone their sectarian bias against Christianity to cooperate in the fight against war and fascism. "Why should we not hope to learn something also from friendly communist neighbors in America?" Coe asked.[124] It was deeply inspiring, he felt, ". . . to observe workingmen, workingwomen, public-school teachers, college professors, Christian ministers, and officers of the communist party in the United States deliberating together in the executive committees as equals."[125] Ward explained that the Communist bias against Christianity was the product of its limited experience with the old European churches; there was no dialectical analysis of religion. If Americans could display a "social revolutionary dynamic" in religion, he was sure that the Communists would speedily have a change of heart. After all, Ward added, it was much better to be allied with Communists than with capitalists who were destroying both religion and society.[126]

[122] Herbert Wilton Stanley, "Red Fascism," *The American Mercury,* XXXVIII (August, 1936), 396.

[123] Harry Frederick Ward, "Christians and Communists," *The Christian Century,* LII (December 25, 1935), 1652.

[124] George Albert Coe, "When Pacifism Turns Sectarian," *The Christian Century,* LII (April 3, 1935), 430.

[125] *Ibid.,* 430.

[126] Harry Frederick Ward, "Christians and Communists," *The Christian Century,* LII (December 25, 1935), 1652.

To the majority of pacifists cooperation with the Communists was heresy. Allan Hunter proposed four serious objections to the "united front": the Communist Party justified any means to achieve its ends; the "united front" experience gave young radicals a temporary thrill but did not lead them into calm and effective action—"The idea seems to be not to produce social engineers, but matadors;"[127] the taint of Communist affiliation damaged the fight against evil and the support of reform movements because it made the individual or group susceptible to the charge that the Communists were behind it; and it inculcated the idea that class war was inevitable.[128] The temptation to join was strong because the goals adopted by the "united front" were admirable; to refuse bred a feeling of guilt.

Kirby Page issued similar warnings that the aims of the Communist Party had not been altered; its aim in the "united front" was to defeat reformist elements and to gain a national audience. Communist strategy of the forceful seizure of power was the antithesis of the pacifist's refusal to sanction either international or class war; "Nothing is to be gained by making a fetish of unity where there is no unity," he concluded.[129] The challenge offered by the "united front" helped to clarify the nature of pacifist thought by pointing up the crucial question of the use of violence in the class struggle. It stimulated a vigorous discussion as reflected in the break in the ranks of the Fellowship of Reconciliation and it helped to segregate and move out of the pacifist ranks those for whom pacifism was simply the means to an end.

Despite the general agreement among the pacifists that they should support peaceful efforts to secure a more just social and economic order and the considerable discussion they expended on the subject, their comments on the practical measures and reforms necessary for such a system were surprisingly sketchy. The one reform that did arouse enthusiasm arose naturally out of pacifist assumptions—penal reform and the abolition of capital punishment. Capital punishment was universally condemned by pacifists because it violated the concept of the supreme value of human life. Several pacifists, moreover, went beyond this position to suggest plans for a better penal system.

Roger Baldwin, director of the American Civil Liberties Union, discussing this problem in great detail, began with this provocative assertion: "I venture to say that no man sentenced to an American prison or jail today, even the best of them, comes out a better man

[127] Allan Armstrong Hunter, "Pacifists and the 'United Front'," *The Christian Century,* LIII (January 8, 1936), 48.

[128] *Ibid.,* 48.

[129] Kirby Page, "What Is Behind the United Front," *The World Tomorrow,* XVI (October 26, 1933), 588.

for his prison experience."[130] The most frequent crimes—those against property—emphasized the failure of our whole social order. The basic reform thus was that of changing the social system. In an article written in 1928, Baldwin lauded the Soviet penology system as a model for the nation to follow. The basic theory of that system that crime is the product either of bad social conditions or diseased minds won his approval. Baldwin described such features as the elimination of the death penalty except for armed robbery and political offenses, the maximum prison sentence of ten years, and the use of farm colonies with the many opportunities for work that were provided. Baldwin's suggestions as to steps that could be taken immediately included the more frequent use of probation and less resort to prison, abolition of capital punishment, juvenile courts, psychiatric examinations, and allowing prisoners more self-government.[131]

Kirby Page and Reinhold Niebuhr pleaded for a more careful classification and separation of prisoners by pointing out the differences between habitual criminals, young criminals, those who committed crime on the spur of the moment, and those who were physically and mentally unfit.[132] The purpose of a penal system was not fulfilled by merely protecting society; it must also be redemptive and thus each of the classes of criminals must be handled differently. Most urgent of all, however, was the reform of the conditions which bred crime—poverty, poor housing, alcohol and drug addiction, commercialized amusements, the breakdown of the home, and mental and physical deficiencies.[133] The concern with problems of crime was not a new one in the pacifist ranks; the great figures of a century before, Dodge, Ladd, Burritt, and Garrison, all had denounced capital punishment.[134]

Apart from the discussion of penology, proposed reforms and the means for effecting them were to a large degree pet projects and ideas of individual pacifists for which there was little, if any, general agreement. In the area of political action, Harry Ward thought the immediate challenge was to defeat anti-sedition bills and bills making it an offense to approach the armed forces with propaganda to influence them to "disaffection and disobedience."[135] Kirby Page urged all to participate in radical political action either through the Democratic or So-

[130] Roger Nash Baldwin, "The Pacifist Attitude to Crime," *The World Tomorrow,* XI (June, 1928), 265.

[131] *Ibid.,* 265-67.

[132] Kirby Page, "Overcoming Crime by Doing Good," *The World Tomorrow,* IX (December, 1926), 264; Reinhold Niebuhr, "Pacifism and the Use of Force," *The World Tomorrow,* XI (May, 1928), 220.

[133] Kirby Page, "Overcoming Crime by Doing Good," *The World Tomorrow,* IX (December, 1926), 265.

[134] Devere Allen, *The Fight for Peace* (New York: The Macmillan Company, 1930), p. 409.

[135] Harry Frederick Ward, "Judgment Day for Pacifists," *The Christian Century,* LII (December 18, 1935), 1621.

cialist parties.[136] Norman Thomas felt that this constructive action could come only through the Socialist Party.[137] Roger Baldwin advocated a new class labor party.[138]

In the economic field, the suggestions were even more heterogeneous. Roger Baldwin envisioned a powerful union movement extended to such outcasts as unskilled labor, women, and aliens, and eventually resulting in an alliance between the farmer and the worker.[139] Scott Nearing proposed a program including guaranteed employment for all adults able to work, a guaranteed minimum supply of food, clothing, shelter, and other necessities to every man, woman, and child, control and development of natural resources for common use, the "social ownership . . . of all socially productive tools and machines," and legislation to regulate health, working hours, and the general welfare of the working classes.[140] Kirby Page offered a program which included the organization and strengthening of cooperatives, support for collective bargaining, a fight against company unions, participation in strikes when there was a clear case of injustice, and a boycott against employers who exploited their workers or practiced racial discrimination.[141] Page was seconded in these ideas by many of the pacifists.

For the reform of social life, the pacifists had little more to suggest than educational efforts to make people aware of the needs of society and to prepare them for the coming social revolution. John Haynes Holmes suggested the formation of cells of devoted social workers within the church, not unlike the old Catholic orders.[142] Many of the pacifists called as well for the end to all racial discrimination. Thus there was no distinct body of thought or general agreement among the pacifists on the application of their faith to social problems, but, rather, their thinking represents a conglomeration of ideas current in the reformist thought of the day.

The concern of the pacifists with the problems of social and economic injustice invigorated and disrupted the course of pacifist thought. Their thought in this area constituted the distinctive note in the pacifism of the inter-war period.

[136] Kirby Page, "A Program for Peace Action," *The Christian Century* LII (May 15, 1925), 636.

[137] Norman Thomas, "Is Peaceful Revolution Possible?" *The World Tomorrow,* XV (September 14, 1932), 251-253.

[138] Roger Nash Baldwin, "Inside or Outside? Two Views on the Relation of Pacifists to Revolutionary Movements. II. Working Outside," *The World Tomorrow,* VII (July, 1924), 203.

[139] *Ibid.,* 203.

[140] Scott Nearing to the Editors of *The World Tomorrow, The World Tomorrow,* VII (October, 1924), 312.

[141] Kirby Page, "A Program for Peace Action," *The Christian Century,* LII (May 15, 1935), 635-636.

[142] John Haynes Holmes, "Can the Church Stop War?" *The World Tomorrow,* XIV (June, 1931), 190.

CHAPTER IV

PACIFISM AND A JUST AND DURABLE PEACE

The most prolific pacifist writer of the inter-war period was Kirby Page, ". . . the most powerful pacifist in America, or probably in the world."[1] Born in Tyler County, Texas, in 1890, Page received his undergraduate training at Drake University and, at various times, pursued graduate studies at the University of Chicago, Columbia University, and Union Theological Seminary. After three years as a student pastor at Monteith, Iowa, from 1912-1915, Page was ordained by the Disciples of Christ Church and was called to a congregation in Chicago in 1915. The following year he left his church to join in the war work of the Y.M.C.A. in the British Isles and France. At the same time he became the personal secretary to Sherwood Eddy, a social evangelist carrying on a speaking mission in army camps in Great Britain and France. Page, continuing as Eddy's secretary until 1918, accompanied him on a tour of China, Japan, and Korea. Page next assumed the pastorate of a church in New York City from 1918 to 1921, but in the latter year he gave up the pulpit for a life-time work as a social evangelist, author, political analyst and agitator, and publicist. For most men pacifism was a belief which was readily tacked on to their other beliefs on political, social, and economic affairs. For Page, pacifism was a life's work; the movement of the inter-war period owed much of its vitality and relevance to his untiring efforts.

Page maintained a close relationship with Sherwood Eddy; together they wrote and published voluminously. From 1926 to 1934 Page edited *The World Tomorrow,* a most remarkable periodical representing pacifist, socialist, and liberal Protestant thought. Founded in 1918 and edited until 1921 by Norman Thomas, the magazine had on its editorial staff during its brief career such notables as John Nevin Sayre, Devere Allen, Paul H. Douglas, Reinhold Niebuhr, and John Haynes Holmes. Page became a contributing editor of *The Christian Century* when *The World Tomorrow* merged with it in 1934. He served as well as a Vice-Chairman of the Fellowship of Reconciliation. World travel occupied much of his time; in 1940 he covered nineteen thousand miles in the United States speaking three times daily against

[1] Sherwood Eddy, *Eighty Adventurous Years: An Autobiography* (New York: Harper and Brothers, 1955), p. 204. (Hereinafter cited as Eddy, *Eighty Adventurous Years.*)

war preparedness.[2] The results of his life-time of observation and thought were over two dozen books translated into many languages relating social religion to contemporary social, economic, and political events.

During the period 1932-1933, Page denounced capitalism and joined the Socialist Party. His was not a revolutionary Marxian socialism but the parliamentarian, evolutionary socialism of English and American development, for Page was a bitter foe of communism. He was greatly interested in developing pacifism as a political technique, but he never lost the conviction that it was also a religious and ethical ideal: ". . . the intrinsic, direct application of the love ethic . . ."[3] pervaded his entire life and thought. He was one of a small number of pacifists who seriously thought out the problems of the actions a pacifist should adopt to build a world of peace.[4]

In 1934 Page outlined in an article entitled, "If War Is to Be Abolished," a five-point program for world peace that summarized much of his thinking on this question.[5] The title itself was indicative of the approach the pacifists made to the problem of peace. Their starting point was the analysis of the nature and causes of war; from this pivot they sought to construct pragmatic social instruments and attitudes that would eliminate war. Thus in a real sense their definition of peace was the absence of war; at least, this was the immediate peace they sought.

In the inter-war period pacifism was often popularly understood as being synonymous with isolationism. In fact, both in attitude and policy the liberal Protestant pacifists were internationalists. The taint of isolationism arose from the opposition the pacifists, together with the isolationists, gave to measures of war preparedness, foreign aid, and intervention from 1935 to 1941.

The first step toward peace outlined by Page was one we have already discussed, for Page believed that the capitalism must be eliminated and replaced by socialism before men could entertain any hope of world understanding. This followed logically from his definition of

[2] Florence R. Flournoy, "The Protestant Churches and the War," *The South Atlantic Quarterly,* XLII (April, 1943), 116.

[3] J. Neal Hughley, *Trends in Protestant Social Idealism* (Morningside Heights, New York: King's Crown Press, 1948), p. 73. (Hereinafter cited as Hughley, *Protestant Social Idealism.*)

[4] Biographical data on Page are drawn from *Who's Who in America: A Biographical Dictionary of Notable Men and Women of the United States* (Chicago: A. N. Marquis Company, 1954), XXI, 1996; Eddy, *Eighty Adventurous Years,* p. 204; Hughley, *Protestant Social Idealism,* pp. 71-88.

[5] Kirby Page, "If War Is to Be Abolished," *The World Tomorrow,* XVII (July 26, 1934), 371-373.

economic imperialism as the cause of war, an imperialism he believed to be inherent in capitalism. If this first step seemed far-reaching and visionary, he quickly turned to specific means of checking the economic causes of war.

The second point in Page's program was the repudiation by the United States of armed intervention in other countries to protect personal and property rights of American citizens. This had long been a favorite idea of the pacifists; no aspect of American foreign relations was under such constant attack as American relationships with the Caribbean nations. The 1927 intervention in Nicaragua, after the United States had previously withdrawn its troops in 1925, was responsible, to a great measure, for the priority given to this aspect of the peace program. In retrospect, no part of the pacifist peace aims was carried out in the public policy of the inter-war period as fully as this idea was in the actions of Harding, Coolidge, Hoover, and in the Good Neighbor policy of Roosevelt. Page asked that the government warn American citizens going abroad that they did so at their own risk and that the government would protect them only by peaceful means. Page called for an "unequivocal repudiation" through legislation of armed intervention on land or sea.[6] Scott Nearing in 1924 desired to go further by replacing the Monroe Doctrine with a "free association" of the nations of the Western Hemisphere.[7] Devere Allen demanded the regulation of the export of surplus capital.[8]

While Page was satisfied with pinpointing this one proposal to meet the threat of the economic imperialism, his fellows considered additional plans revealing clearly this internationalist orientation. The reduction or elimination of tariff barriers was recommended by many pacifists, including Luccock, Fosdick, Niebuhr, Palmer, Sayre, Thomas, Tittle, Allen, and Villard. Norman Thomas desired at the most a limited use of tariffs while calling on the United States in 1931 to take the lead in sponsoring an international economic conference to bring about general readjustments.[9] Scott Nearing desired a similar conference to abolish all tariffs, trade and passport restrictions, and all other barriers to free intercourse among nations.[10] The pacifists assumed that freedom defined as the

[6] *Ibid.*, 372; Kirby Page, "A New National Preparedness," *The Forum,* LXXXI (February, 1929), 74.

[7] Scott Nearing to the Editors of *The World Tomorrow, The World Tomorrow,* VII (October, 1924), 312.

[8] Devere Allen, "War Resistance as War Prevention," *The World Tomorrow,* XII (January, 1929), 12.

[9] Norman Thomas, "Removing Economic Barriars to Peace," *The World Tomorrow,* XIV (November, 1931), 359.

[10] Scott Nearing to the Editors of *The World Tomorrow, The World Tomorrow,* VII (October, 1924), 311.

absence of restriction would in and of itself foster prosperity and good will among the nations; they believed that restrictions were the product of antiquated thinking in an interdependent world rather than the reflection of deep-seated national policies.

Prompted by the notion that war resulted from the struggle for raw materials and markets, pacifists called for "free access" to raw materials. Just what was meant by "free access" was not at all clear. Perhaps they had in mind a program like that of Thomas, Allen, and Villard which contained provisions for an international administration or an economic commission of experts to regulate the world's supplies of raw materials.[11]

Pacifists were similarly ambiguous when they talked of "free access" to markets and "readjustments" in the administration and control of colonies. They most often meant not "freedom" as such, but a form of international control guaranteeing an equality of opportunity to all nations. The international conference was the favored *modus operandi.* Villard, for example, desired an international discussion of the colonial system to effect a new method of control.[12] There were numerous other suggestions for conferences to deal with specific problems or the general economic situation. Kirby Page thought in 1928 (before his switch to socialism) that the industrialists and financiers of the world ought to meet regularly as they had during the International Chamber of Commerce sessions in 1919.[13] In 1938 after the Munich experience, Albert Palmer issued an appeal for a world conference to consider the economic necessities behind Hitler's aggressions with the hope of stabilizing world peace in terms of the Munich pacts. Palmer suggested that if the governments ignored his appeal, the Federal Council of Churches should contact religious bodies throughout the world to bring pressure to bear upon their governments.[14] Two months prior to Munich, Villard had made a similar plea.[15]

Villard, Nearing, and Thomas, however, went beyond the conference idea and pictured an international control of economic life.[16] Thomas

[11] Norman Thomas, "Removing Economic Barriers to Peace," *The World Tomorrow,* XIV (November, 1931), 358; Devere Allen, "War Resistance as War Prevention," *The World Tomorrow,* XII (January, 1929), 12; Oswald Garrison Villard, "Issues and Men," *The Nation,* CXLVII (July 2, 1938), 18.

[12] Oswald Garrison Villard, "Issues and Men," *The Nation,* CXLVII (July 2, 1938), 18.

[13] Kirby Page, "International Economic Cooperation," *The World Tomorrow,* XII (September, 1929), 372.

[14] Albert Wentworth Palmer, "Call a World Economic Conference!" *The Christian Century,* LV (November 9, 1938), 1368-1369.

[15] Oswald Garrison Villard, "Issues and Men," *The Nation,* CXLVII (July 2, 1938), 18.

[16] Oswald Garrison Villard, "Gentlemen May Cry Peace," *The Saturday Review of Literature,* XI (April 6, 1935), 596; Scott Nearing to the Editors of

proposed a world commission of experts, similar to the group governing the supplies of raw materials, to direct an international fiscal system. The origins of these commissions and their relationship to other organs of international authority were not clear in the limited discussion Thomas and the others gave of their plans. What was clear, however, was that the pacifists were internationalist in their approach to world affairs, desiring to efface the dogmas and restrictions of nationalism.

The third step on Page's path to peace was disarmament. This was a key clause in every pacifist peace program, and the popularity of the idea persists into present-day peace planning. Disarmament was a direct attempt to meet the theory that war was the result, at least the immediate result, of the friction and fear caused by armament races and war preparedness arising out of the demands of the balance of power system. Pacifists called for "total," "complete," "universal," or "full" disarmament; the use of armed forces for any purpose was contrary to their basic presuppositions. Luccock talked of "progressive" disarmament and Sayre proposed a time-table system of reduction to the point where no rapid mobilization was possible.[17]

Pacifists reiterated unceasingly that armaments failed to provide security. Armaments instead created hostility, for, in order to interest the public in a program of war preparedness, it was first necessary to arouse suspicion of other nations; the creation of suspicion and fear set in motion the forces that led inevitably to war. Armaments, moreover, failed to bring material prosperity; they were a "bottomless hole" in the national economy into which were poured the valuable resources of a nation which could have been used for programs of social and economic development. For pacifists were sure that any dispute could be settled in a more friendly and economical manner than to resort to arms. Their prize, and oft-repeated, illustration of this was the friendship between Canada and the United States since the Rush-Bagot Treaty of 1817 which left the boundary line between the two nations unarmed.[18]

John Haynes Holmes pointed out that disarmament was essential to the outlawry of war program; there was a distressing irony in the fact of nations outlawing war on one day and passing cruiser bills on the

---

The World Tomorrow, The World Tomorrow, VII (October, 1924), 311; Norman Thomas, "War, Politics and Economics," *The World Tomorrow,* V (January, 1922), 10-12.

[17] Halford Edward Luccock, "Religion and World Crisis," *The World Tomorrow,* XIV (November, 1931), 366; John Nevin Sayre, "The Disarmament Objective," *The World Tomorrow,* XV (February, 1932), 40.

[18] Kirby Page, "Why Disarmament?" *The World Tomorrow,* XIV (November, 1931), 346-348.

next.[19] Sayre was quite sure that if the United States would take the lead in disarmament, other nations would be led, not to acts of aggression against the United States, but to friendly relations without the fear that haunted the relations between armed nations.[20] The vital question as to how the disarmament was to be effected, however, remained largely unanswered. Except for Sayre's nebulous time-table plan and the suggestions for further disarmament conferences made by Nearing in 1924 and Villard in 1938, the question was ignored by the pacifist writers.[21]

The theory of mitigating the terror and destruction of warfare by banning weapons or methods of warfare through international law and treaty agreement met with no response from this generation of pacifists with the exception of Villard who proposed, as late as 1938, a ban on bombers and submarines.[22] An attempt to ban poison gas by law in terms of the Geneva protocol of 1925 was defeated in Congress in 1926; after that time pacifists seem to have accepted the view that in time of war nations will use whatever means are suited to their ends and that the only sensible course of action is to prevent the outbreak of war itself. This was the argument Allen advanced against the idea of an international ban on poison gas, though he did see as well a psychological value in such a ban as a token of a revolt against the war system and of the power of a nation with a high chemical productivity to subordinate that interest to the general welfare.[23]

Closely allied to the ban on weapons was the proposal advanced by Otto Glaser, a professor of biology at Amherst College, that scientists refuse to do research on bombs, poison gas, or projectiles in peace time. Scientists, supposedly pacifistic and internationally-minded by nature, should adopt an oath resembling the Hippocratic oath and band together with an international labor organization so that they would be able to strike effectively, if need be, to protect their persecuted members.[24] Albert Einstein in 1931, unaware that his own creative genius was to make possible the most destructive weapons in human history, challenged scientists in a similar fashion to refuse to do research for war

[19] John Haynes Holmes, "Outlawry of War—A Policy of Abolition," *The World Tomorrow,* IX (November, 1926), 207.

[20] John Nevin Sayre, "Pacifism and National Security," *The World Tomorrow,* XI (August, 1928), 331.

[21] Scott Nearing to the Editors of *The World Tomorrow, The World Tomorrow,* VII (October, 1924), 311; Oswald Garrison Villard, "Issues and Men," *The Nation,* CXLVII (July 2, 1938), 18.

[22] Oswald Garrison Villard, "Issues and Men," *The Nation,* CXLVII (July 2, 1938), 18.

[23] Devere Allen, "The Ban on Poison Gas," *The World Tomorrow,* X (January, 1927), 25.

[24] Otto Glaser, "Science and the War Against War," *The World Tomorrow,* VII (February, 1924), 46.

purposes.[25] These suggestions, however, made little headway even into the peace plans of the pacifists.

The building of an international legal and political structure to make possible the peaceful settlement of disputes had a potent appeal to pacifists. Page placed as the fourth step on his program the strengthening of all international agencies of justice. The refusal of the United States to enter the League or the World Court dampened the pacifists' enthusiasm by the mid-thirties, but they never rejected the idea or the vision. The pacifists believed that if only war came to be thought of as illegal and if only an international framework were provided to which the nations were committed, peace would be a reality. Treaties of arbitration and conciliation were the favorite items of peace programs prior to the First World War. That interest persisted throughout the inter-war period, but it was enlarged to embrace a far-reaching program of international cooperation.

The pacifists quite sensibly pledged their support first of all to the existing international agencies; they felt, despite many reservations, that it was best to begin with what they had. Villard, in fact, asserted that the success of international agencies must be assured before steps could be taken to insure economic justice.[26] Most pacifists gave strong support to efforts to bring the United States into the League of Nations. William Hull believed that at least the United States should cooperate with the League commissions.[27] While Villard was a major critic of the original League from the day it was written into the Versailles Treaty, he warmly supported the concept of an international agency and called for the organization of a new "democratic" league.[28] Page's poll of Protestant ministers in 1931 found sixty-six per cent in favor of immediate entry into the League.[29] Allen was much more cautious in asking whether the League, controlled by Great Britain, France, Belgium, and Italy, the same nations that went to war, could be relied upon. He thought that supporting the international labor movement offered greater assurance to the pacifists.[30]

The principal reservations the pacifists entered against the League

[25] *The Christian Century,* XLVIII (September 2, 1931), 1085.

[26] Oswald Garrison Villard, "Gentlemen May Cry Peace," *The Saturday Review of Literature,* XI (April 6, 1935), 596.

[27] William Isaac Hull, "The League of Nations: Shall the United States Enter It?" *The World Tomorrow,* V (November, 1922), 336.

[28] Oswald Garrison Villard, "Issues and Men," *The Nation,* CXLVII (July 2, 1938), 18.

[29] Kirby Page, "Nineteen Thousand Clergymen on War and Peace," *The World Tomorrow,* XIV (May, 1931), 140.

[30] Devere Allen, "Prerequisites of Peace," *The World Tomorrow,* V (November, 1922), 327.

of Nations involved the question of sanctions, for here the pacifists faced the problem of what degree of coercion they were willing to consider ethical. There was no dissent as to the ethical character of diplomatic sanctions such as the withdrawal of the diplomatic corps from a nation or the refusal to carry on the customary relations. Pacifists advocated the use of this type of sanction against Japan in 1932.

On the question of economic sanctions, however, there was a considerable range of opinion. Page supported financial and economic pressure including an official embargo but excluding the blockade or boycott, for he saw in the latter the means of inflicting suffering upon the innocent as well as the guilty and of running the risk of war.[31] Sayre and Villard gave vigorous endorsement to economic sanctions; Villard late in the thirties talked of the wisdom of Britain and France applying a complete economic sanction on Germany as a means of bringing Hitler to his senses.[32] Allen changed his mind during the period from the endorsement of the blockade in 1924 to the rejection of it during the Manchurian crisis of 1932. At that time he said, that no nation in the world had the right to judge another nation as the European powers were doing to Japan, for none was impartial. A blockade would bring suffering to the innocent of Japan; there was a definite risk of a declaration of war by Japan. Allen continued to give his support to the popular, unofficial boycott by the citizens of a nation.[33] Niebuhr held that economic sanctions had a higher ethical justification than military sanctions but that they were a more dangerous expedient than most pacifists were willing to admit.[34] It was upon this very question in relation to Italy's attack on Ethiopia that Sherwood Eddy took the stand that led him away from the pacifist faith, for he supported not only economic sanctions against Italy but also their enforcement by the naval forces of Great Britain and France under the direction of the League in case of an armed attack of retaliation by Italy.[35]

This discussion furnishes a good example of the pacifist attempt to measure every possible alternative action in the light of an absolutistic position, instead of waiting to judge the efficacy and ethics of an action in terms of an actual historical situation. While Eddy supported military

[31] Kirby Page, "Pacifism and International Police," *The World Tomorrow,* XI (June, 1928), 259.

[32] John Nevin Sayre, "Pacifism and National Security," *The World Tomorrow,* XI (August, 1928), 332; Oswald Garrison Villard, "Issues and Men," *The Nation,* CXLVIII (March 25, 1939), 350.

[33] Devere Allen, "Youth Movements Face the Future," *The World Tomorrow,* VII (May, 1924), 149; Devere Allen to the Editors of *The World Tomorrow, The World Tomorrow,* XV (June, 1932), 189-190.

[34] Reinhold Niebuhr, "Pacifism and the Use of Force," *The World Tomorrow,* XI (May, 1928), 218.

[35] Sherwood Eddy to the Editor of *The Christian Century, The Christian Century,* LII (December 11, 1935), 1594.

sanctions in the Italian question and felt that pacifism no longer fit the historical alternatives, Page and his fellow pacifists remained faithful to their refusal to give way to the war system. Niebuhr in 1928 repeated the pacifist adages that there exists no impartial judge of the nations and that the League no more than any single nation could wage war without destroying the innocent.[36] Ten years later he was in the vanguard of those who wished to stand up to Hitler even if it meant another holocaust.

Page explored still another variation on the theme: the development of world public opinion as a sanction against war. Using his favorite analogy of the United States Supreme Court, Page observed that the court in decisions affecting state governments never attempted to use any form of physical coercion to enforce its decisions, but rested always on the power of public opinion within the state to insure compliance. This was the only force, he believed, that could halt the aggressive action of a great power or an alliance of powers.[37]

While the pacifists' discussion of sanctions had solid basis in the contemporary scene for the Manchurian and Ethiopian crises made necessary League decisions on the use of sanctions, their discussions of an international police force were purely theoretical. The issues involved here differed from that of military sanctions. The pacifists had accepted the domestic police force as a necessary instrument for maintaining civil order; they justified their stand on the grounds that a body of law existed and that the police were impartial administrators of that law, not parties to the dispute. What violence did occur in enforcing the law was directed at the guilty, not the innocent. There were a few pacifists—Albert Day, Georgia Harkness, and Harry Emerson Fosdick—who supported the idea of an international police force because they accepted the analogy between the domestic and international police as a valid one, assuming that an international tribunal with world-wide authority were created.[38]

Kirby Page, however, had his doubts and countered the proposal with his handy analogy of the Supreme Court. In cases involving individuals, the Court would use the Federal and state governments to enforce its decisions, but between states it relied upon the power of public

[36] Reinhold Niebuhr, "Pacifism and the Use of Force," *The World Tomorrow,* XI (May, 1928), 218.

[37] Kirby Page, "Pacifism and International Police," *The World Tomorrow,* XI (June, 1928), 258.

[38] Albert Edward Day, "If America Is Drawn into War, Can You, As a Christian, Participate in It or Support It?" *The Christian Century,* LVII (December 25, 1940), 1611; Georgia Harkness, "What Can Christians Do?" *The Christian Century,* LVII (May 29, 1940), 700; Harry Emerson Fosdick, "If America Is Drawn into War, Can You, As a Christian, Participate in It or Support It?" *The Christian Century,* LVIII (January 22, 1941), 115.

opinion. The analogy between states long united and in subordination to a federal government and sovereign nations belonging to an international organization might well appear far-fetched, but Page had a practical argument as well which carried more weight. War, he said, involved alliances of nations with which no international police force could hope to cope.[39] Sayre, anticipating Page's Supreme Court analogy by using it to state his objections to the hypothetical international police force, stated that the actions of nations under League direction could not be considered as international police action because they were the result, not of an impartial tribunal, but of the decisions of the very nations involved in the issues at hand.[40]

Pacifists sought the creation of an international court of law capable of rendering decisions in all disputes subject to the law. Before the First World War, they had been zealous supporters of the Permanent Court of Arbitration. After the war, they endorsed the entry of the United States into the World Court. This was another situation when Page felt it was best to begin with what was already in existence. John Haynes Holmes and William Hull pressed for entry with the acceptance of the compulsory jurisdiction clause.[41] The complementary idea of a codification of international law received little attention. Allen included it in his description of the necessary steps to erect a legal structure to prevent war, but that was the extent of pacifist thought on the subject.[42]

The traditional pacifist emphases on arbitration and conciliation continued in full force. These had formed part of its program since the days of William Ladd and had dominated its thought at the turn of the century. These plans were an integral part of the legal approach which sought to impose law and order upon the international community. Allen and Page called for "effective agencies" of arbitration and conciliation.[43] Palmer wanted a world council on conciliation, but the task he desired this council to perform was more grandiose than mere conciliation, for he envisioned a plan for a world government or organiza-

[39] Kirby Page, "Pacifism and International Police," *The World Tomorrow,* XI (June, 1928), 258-261.

[40] John Nevin Sayre, "Disarmament and Defense," *The World Tomorrow,* V (January, 1922), 3-4.

[41] John Haynes Holmes, "Outlawry of War—A Policy of Abolition," *The World Tomorrow,* IX (November, 1926), 207; William Isaac Hull, "The League of Nations: Shall the United States Enter It?" *The World Tomorrow,* V (November, 1922), 337.

[42] Devere Allen, "War Resistance as War Prevention," *The World Tomorrow,* XII (January, 1929), 12.

[43] *Ibid.,* 12; Kirby Page, "But Evil Must Be Conquered," *The World Tomorrow,* IX (October, 1926), 169; Kirby Page, "Pacifism and International Police," *The World Tomorrow,* XI (June, 1928), 259.

tion that all nations could accept "without humiliation." The council was to be composed, not of diplomats—here Palmer gave vent to the American suspicion of the subtle arts of that craft—but by the best "brains" from all over the world.[44] Sayre, as well, considered the demands for arbitration and conciliation, and he added his proposal for both treaties and tribunals to put them into effect.[45] Thus arbitration and conciliation were still integral parts of the pacifist peace program.

The attraction that the idea of the international conferences had for the pacifists has already been noted; some further illustrations suggest the potency of the idea. Page proposed not only the international conferences of financiers and business men but regular conferences of workers as well. Pointing out the number of large international labor organizations already in existence, he pictured the force and influence they would exert by uniting to discuss their common aims. Page was also enthusiastic about regular international governmental conferences such as the International Economic Conference of 1927. There were three significant values, he declared, to be gained from such affairs: the research and documentation done in preparation constituted an invaluable source of information; the recommendations of these conferences exerted a strong influence on world public opinion; and the personal contact between men from all over the world aided in creating friendship among nations.[46] Though Page was naively optimistic about the influence of world conferences, his ideas appear coldly realistic beside the dream of Villard when he suggested in 1935 that the Allies of the First World War should call the nations of the world together, admit the failures of the peace they had made at Versailles, and offer to work out a new permament arrangement with guarantees of justice to the defeated powers of the World War.[47] The attraction of the conference idea provided a temptation for the pacifists because it was so easy to confuse the demand for calling a conference with the belief that once in session the conference would successfully deal with the problems placed before it. The conference idea had the appearance of progressive action, but the pacifist in advocating it often minimized or ignored the scope and complexity of the problems for which he desired a solution.

Other international organizations received the endorsement of some pacifists. Page and *The World Tomorrow* urged the United States to

[44] Albert Wentworth Palmer, "If America Is Drawn into War, Can You, As a Christian, Participate in It or Support It?" *The Christian Century,* LVIII (January 8, 1941), 53.

[45] John Nevin Sayre, "Pacifism and National Security," *The World Tomorrow,* XI (August, 1928), 332.

[46] Kirby Page, "International Economic Cooperation," *The World Tomorrow,* XII (September, 1929), 372-373.

[47] Oswald Garrison Villard, "Gentlemen May Cry Peace," *The Saturday Review of Literature,* XI (April 6, 1935), 595.

join the International Labor Organization;[48] Villard continued to press for greater cooperation with this group after the United States became a member in 1934.[49] Page and Sayre asked for full American cooperation with the Pan-American Union.[50] Thomas added his request for the support of all international and national consumers' cooperative movements.[51]

There was a widespread demand for revision of the Versailles Treaty and, more specifically, for the reduction or cancellation of the war reparations with a similar accompanying action on the allied war loans. Thomas thought an international conference on this problem could end the ". . . folly of trying to make the present and the future by some hocus-pocus pay the past costs of a cruel, stupid, and unnecessary imperialist war in which no one nation was the sole offender."[52] The one condition he demanded was that the cancellation should not result in any increase in armaments.[53] It is interesting to note, however, that the demands by Luccock, Niebuhr, Thomas, and Nearing on the question of reparations did not appear until 1931. In no sense can it be said that the pacifists led public opinion in this request. Niebuhr desired that the interrelationship between the debts and loans be officially recognized; he castigated them as "pure tribute" in a world economically interdependent.[54] Robert Herrick and Devere Allen voiced the sentiments of most pacifists when they called for a "divorce" of the League from the responsibility of enforcing the Versailles arrangement.[55]

In 1931, a year that challenged pacifists to basic rethinking of international problems, Niebuhr and Thomas called for the recognition of Russia and the reopening of trade. Thomas saw this as the only alternative to an all-out war to destroy the Soviet Union. Trade, it was hoped, would relieve the tension, fear, and hostility created within Russia by her isolation at the hands of the Western world.[56] Albert

[48] Kirby Page, "Pacifism and International Police," *The World Tomrorow,* XI (June, 1928), 259.

[49] Oswald Garrison Villard, "Issues and Men," *The Nation,* CXLVII (July 2, 1938), 18.

[50] Kirby Page, "Pacifism and International Police," *The World Tomorrow,* XI (June, 1928), 259.

[51] Norman Thomas, "Can Pacifism Act Against Injustice?" *The World Tomorrow,* VII (July, 1924), 210.

[52] Norman Thomas, "Removing Economic Barriers to Peace," *The World Tomorrow,* XIV (November, 1931), 359.

[53] *Ibid.,* 359.

[54] Reinhold Niebuhr, "Economic Perils to World Peace," *The World Tomorrow,* XIV (May, 1931), 155.

[55] Robert Herrick, "The War and Ourselves," *The Survey,* LII (August 1, 1924), 525; Devere Allen, "Prerequisites of Peace," *The World Tomorrow,* V (November, 1922), 327.

[56] Reinhold Niebuhr, "Making Peace with Russia," *The World Tomorrow,* XIV (November, 1931), 354-355; Norman Thomas, "Removing Economic Barriers to Peace," *The World Tomorrow,* XIV (November, 1931), 359.

Guerard, criticizing the tenor of much of the thinking in pacifist circles regarding the injustice of peace settlements, prophetically warned in 1933 that the nations should not encourage or agree to territorial changes for Germany, for he contended that territorial injustice was a lesser evil than the injustice of the war that would follow if changes were once begun.[57] Pacifist thinking on international questions, then, reflected current trends of the day, and though it occasionally differed in the weight of emphasis placed on one solution or one idea, it was in no way distinctive, nor could the advocacy of these ideas be attributed to the pacifists alone.

One aspect of the legalistic approach to war prevention, not mentioned by Page in 1934, had received his enthusiastic support a few years earlier. The outlawry of war movement was an amazing phenomenon in the history of the peace movement. As Robert Ferrell has said, ". . . by the spring of 1927 no one peace formula had appeared in the United States capable of uniting enthusiastically all the various American peace groups."[58] But within a year all were united in support of the outlawry of war. This idea, a pet notion of Solmon O. Levinson, a wealthy Chicago lawyer, was given official corporate form as the American Committee for Outlawry of War in 1921, in the leadership of which Levinson was assisted by John Dewey, Charles Clayton Morrison, the editor of *The Christian Century,* and John Haynes Holmes. After winning an alliance with Senator Borah, chairman of the Senate Committee on Foreign Relations, the organization campaigned to win popular support for the program.[59]

Holmes noted that the pacifists first treated the plan as naive, as a meaningless panacea. The outlawry of war concept demanded a new mode of thought, he suggested, for it attempted to cut right through all the plans for controlling and regulating war, all the attempts to get at the causes of war by simply stating that henceforth war was illegal. Essential to the concept was a world-wide condemnation of war in public opinion. Holmes was sure that this state of public opinion already existed as a result of the experience of the First World War. To outlaw war thus was simply officially to rule illegal what was already condemned by the people. Holmes pointed to the American experience with various social evils, e.g., slavery and prostitution. The attempt to control or regulate had always failed, with a resulting loss of dignity

[57] Albert Guerard to the Editor of *The New Republic, The New Republic,* LXXV (June 7, 1933), 103.

[58] Robert H. Ferrell, *Peace in Their Time: The Origins of the Kellogg-Briand Pact* (New Haven: Yale University Press, 1952), p. 16. (Hereinafter cited as Ferrell, *Peace in Their Time.*)

[59] *Ibid.,* pp. 31-36; L. Ethan Ellis. *Frank B. Kellogg and American Foreign Relations, 1925-1929* (New Brunswick, New Jersey. Rutgers University Press. 1961), pp. 193-212.

and respect suffered by the whole community. The "American way" was to abolish the evil by law. Holmes warned that ruling war illegal would not end war immediately. A world court and disarmament were essential prerequisites for peace, but the basic act was accomplished when the people's condemnation of war was given legal verification.[60]

It is difficult today to recapture the confident faith given this plan in 1928 and 1929, but it is reflected in the writing of the pacifists through 1930 when, it would seem, the successive challenges to the peace structure made by Japan, Italy, and Germany awakened its adherents, including the pacifists, to the awareness that the assumed world condemnation of war was an illusion and that the Kellogg-Briand Pact which had represented the signal triumph of the peace movement in the twenties was powerless in a rearming world. Page in 1926 declared that outlawry was essential to a realization of permanent peace; in 1929 he dismissed the many reservations tacked on to the pact as inconsequential because war itself had been declared illegal once and for all.[61] Ferrell concludes that the outlawry of war idea ". . . shows that American popular understanding of the great problems and policies of post-1918 international affairs was appallingly naive."[62]

An offshoot of the outlawry movement was the attempt to obtain a constitutional amendment prohibiting the United States from going to war. Sponsored by the Women's Peace Union, and introduced in the Senate in 1926 and again in 1930 by Senator Lynn Frazier of North Dakota, the proposed amendment stated: "War for any purpose shall be illegal, and neither the United States nor any State, Territory, association, or persons subject to its jurisdiction shall prepare for, declare, engage in, or carry on war or other armed conflict, expedition, invasion, or undertaking within or without the United States, nor shall any funds be issued, appropriated, or expended for such purpose."[63] By 1930 this amendment had gained the backing of the Women's International League for Peace and Freedom, the Fellowship of Reconciliation, the War Resisters' League, the Women's Peace Society, the Peace Section of the American Friends Service Committee, and the Pennsylvania Committee for Total Disarmament.[64] As noted in a previous chapter, Niebuhr alone among the pacifists in the twenties saw what he regarded as the psychological weakness of programs designed to outlaw war; he argued that they were dangerously illusory because they were

[60] John Haynes Holmes, "Outlawry of War—A Policy of Abolition," *The World Tomorrow,* IX (November, 1926), 204-207.

[61] Kirby Page, "Overcoming Evil with Good in International Affairs," *The World Tomorrow,* IX (November, 1926), 215; Kirby Page, "A New National Preparedness," *The Forum,* LXXXI (February, 1929), 74.

[62] Ferrell, *Peace in Their Time,* pp. 264-265.

[63] *The World Tomorrow,* XIII (May, 1930), 197.

[64] *Ibid.,* p. 197.

based on trust alone and beguiled ". . . a nation which stands aloof to preserve the advantages of its strength into believing that it stands aloof to preserve the advantages of its virtue."[65]

One final aspect of pacifist thought on the legal framework for a peaceful world involved proposals for world organization and world government. There was a singular unanimity about its thought on this subject. In 1922 Sayre outlined a plan for a world "association" of nations including such provisions as open diplomacy, "democratic control," a world court, and enforcement by public opinion rather than by a police force.[66] Sayre's "association" was vaguely conceived and left undefined the form or shape the association would assume. Page sharpened the concept considerably in a plan outlined in 1926 which called for a federal world government patterned on the United States Constitution. Page's proposal provided for a permanent representative body where all nations would confer regularly; an international administrative body to execute the decisions of the legislature; and an international tribunal to interpret the meaning of agreements and to settle legal disputes.[67] Page declared further in 1928 that the real executive was to be public opinion, for he opposed any idea of international armed forces as being unnecessary and impractical.[68] This plan was essentially a restatement of William Ladd's "Congress of Nations" plan drawn up in 1840.

After Page had drawn his blueprints in the twenties, there was little discussion of world government until 1940 when Georgia Harkness, Albert Palmer, and A. J. Muste in the face of renewed conflict turned their thoughts to the kind of world they desired at the conclusion of the Second World War.[69] They endorsed the federal principle and clearly rejected the idea of a supergovernment. At no time did they propose the end to the nation-state as the basic unit of international society. The essential note in all of these considerations regarding a legal structure to preserve peace was the insistence that these plans rest ultimately on enforcement by public opinion, on feelings of trust and faith-

[65] Reinhold Niebuhr, "A Critique of Pacifism," *The Atlantic Monthly,* CXXXIX (May, 1927), 641.

[66] John Nevin Sayre, "Disarmament and Defense," *The World Tomorrow,* V (January, 1922), 3.

[67] Kirby Page, "Overcoming Evil with Good in International Affairs," *The World Tomorrow,* IX (November, 1926), 215.

[68] Kirby Page, "Pacifism and International Police," *The World Tomorrow,* XI (June, 1928), 258-261.

[69] Georgia Harkness, "What Can Christians Do?" *The Christian Century,* LVII (May 29, 1940), 700; Albert Wentworth Palmer, "If America Is Drawn into War, Can You, As a Christian, Participate in It, or Support It?" *The Christian Century,* LVIII (January 8, 1941), 52; A. J. Muste to the Editor of *The Christian Century, The Christian Century,* LVII (September 11, 1940), 1117.

fulness among nations. Some would go as far as to endorse economic sanctions or even an international police force if a system of world law were perfected, but enforcement by the military power of the nations was considered a violation of the pacifist's understanding of the nature of war.

There was little in the pacifist thinking about peace as described above that was distinctively a reflection of pacifism; each of the proposals was widely held by other groups in American society. Nevertheless, the fifth and final item in Kirby Page's peace program was maintained by pacifists alone. It was the principle of war resistance; ". . . the sacrament of martydom—to die rather than sin."[70] It was a principle that distinctively marked the pacifist revival following the First World War. While the problem of the international peace structure occupied a few, war resistance concerned all. It offered a course of action for everyone; it was not mere theorizing about hypothetical situations. It was an act that hopefully would be felt and noticed by the government; it was a moral and dramatic equivalent for war because it demanded the highest inner courage and heroism to defy the ordinances of one's own government. In modern war the state demanded and needed the services of all its citizens; the pacifist reasoned that his protest would be a potent one if he could only persuade enough to follow him.

Pacifists interpreted the refusal to participate in war as a new code of international conduct; in fact, a very significant change in terminology symbolized this change in perspective. Instead of "conscientious objection," the pacifists spoke of "war resistance" as a positive action with peacetime implications of seeking to do away with war and refusing to contribute in any way to those acts of government that lead to war.

The experience of war resistance during the First World War was not an encouraging heritage, but developments in the inter-war period were heartening. Of the twenty thousand inducted in the American armed forces who claimed non-combatant status in the First World War only four thousand maintained their position when they reached the army camps.[71] Yet with the return of peace the idea gained new vitality. The War Resisters' International spread rapidly through Europe and the United States, and, though not large in numbers, it made an impact in those countries of Europe where peacetime conscription was practised. From South Africa and India came stirring examples

[70] John Haynes Holmes, "What Anyone Can Do," *The World Tomorrow,* VII (February, 1924), 56.

[71] Mulford Q. Sibley and Philip E. Jacob, *Conscription of Conscience: The American State and the Conscientious Objector, 1940-1947* (Ithaca: Cornell University Press, 1952), p. 12.

of the power of mass disobedience; from the European labor movement came strong resolutions of resistance to war. The Ponsonby Peace Letter, the Peace Pledge Union, and a comparable German pledge signed by more than 300,000 persons seemed to indicate that war resistance had moved beyond the stage of a scattered heroic individual objection to war to a mass popular refusal to sanction war.

Albert Einstein caught the imagination and raised the hopes of pacifists with his simple assertion that if two per cent of the world's population pledged themselves to refuse to participate in war there could be no war because the jails of the world could not accommodate the disloyal two per cent.[72] As "2 per cent" clubs, badges, and feathers multiplied, pacifists began to see a glimmer of the promised land of peace. Einstein instructed pacifists to seek international agreements that would guarantee recognition by the national governments of the status of war resister. War resisters, he continued, should seek difficult tasks to perform in peacetime as an evidence to the world of the sincerity of their convictions; they should band together on the international level—in a sense, the first world citizens.[73] Ernest Fremont Tittle asked that provisions be made whereby war resisters could enroll in peacetime so that there could be no questioning of their intentions when the war clouds formed.[74] Chester Williams, reflecting sarcastically on the military training programs in high schools and colleges, proposed a training program for pacifists which included the counting and assigning of jail accommodations, practicing standing before the firing squad, frequent worship and prayer to gather courage and inspiration, and the rehearsal of the military trials so that the resisters would be prepared with all the correct replies.[75] For some reason mass pledges were not utilized by American pacifists. Nevertheless, war resistance as an idea was the strongest and most widely accepted item of the pacifist peace program.

The pacifists were sanguine about the results of their program of war resistance. Page and Allen predicted that if an "appreciable minority" of Christians or citizens in the United States would refuse to fight, war could not be waged successfully.[76] An announced stand of war resistance had educational value as well, for it forced others to think the matter through; it spead the conviction that war was im-

[72] Albert Einstein, "Militant Pacifism," *The World Tomorrow,* XIV (January, 1931), 9.

[73] *Ibid.,* 9.

[74] Ernest Fremont Tittle, "Preaching and Practicing Peace," *The Christian Century,* LII (April 3, 1935), 443.

[75] Chester S. Williams, "Fire Drill for Pacifists," *The World Tomorrow,* XIV (October, 1931), 323.

[76] Kirby Page, "Shall We Sign the Pacifist Pledge? Yes!" *The Christian Century,* LII (December 11, 1935), 1590; Devere Allen, "War Resistance as War Prevention," *The World Tomorrow,* XII (January, 1929), 14.

moral. Muste saw a practical social result in the weakening of the armed forces through such a refusal to serve, for the military, he contended, was most often employed, not in international conflict, but against labor.[77]

The pacifists had to defend themselves against a number of serious charges and questions regarding war resistance. The first was that of loyalty to the government. Pacifists replied that they were not anarchists in opposing the decisions of the state, for the people were the true government and war was seldom desired by a majority of the people; they were, they assured themselves, ". . . the lingering popular conscience. . . ."[78] They proclaimed a doctrine of "higher loyalty" to society, humanity, the moral law, or to God. The state could not be equated with any of these. The state should be careful, they warned, about destroying innovators, for they provide the path to progress.

The most frequent and seemingly persuasive criticism against the pacifist pledge was that this meant committing oneself to a course of action before the facts were available, before the particular situation could be assessed and the best course of action adopted. The pacifist replied with the statement: "Once a war is imminent, there are no facts accessible . . .," because emotions, propaganda, and censorship made it impossible for the citizen to determine the rational course of action.[79] The pacifist answer had an either/or quality that pervaded all its thinking; thus if one can not have all the facts, then it is better to take a stand on none except the general abhorrence of war.

The same quality characterized its reply to the charge that they were neglecting those that needed protection. The pacifist simply replied that war protected no one. The pacifists recognized, none the less, that although no one could escape giving aid to the war effort or sharing in its results, there was less guilt implicit in indirect aid than in direct aid.[80] On the affirmative side the pacifists claimed that war resistance would reduce international tensions, that it would impel governments toward peace because they would no longer be able to rely on the populace heeding the call to war. It would cut at the roots the reliance upon war as the means of last resort in international politics.[81]

Devere Allen outlined the necessary steps the American war resistance movement would have to take if it were to prevent the nation from

[77] A. J. Muste, "Fight the Good Fight?" *The American Scholar,* VI (Summer, 1937), 338.

[78] Devere Allen, "War Resistance as War Prevention," *The World Tomorrow,* XII (January, 1929), 14.

[79] *Ibid.,* 14.

[80] Kirby Page, "Shall We Sign the Pacifist Pledge? Yes!" *The Christian Century,* LII (December 11, 1935), 1589.

[81] Devere Allen, "War Resistance as War Prevention," *The World Tomorrow,* XII (January, 1929), 15.

going to war. He believed it was necessary to build the movement up to parity with Great Britain, especially in the use of peace pledges, to use more speakers and more literature in the "scientific spirit," to unify its scattered ranks, to increase aid to the War Resisters' International, and, finally, to develop techniques of mobilizing more effectively the forces of war resistance both in times of war and peace.[82] War resistance thus was the one element of the pacifists' peace program that was distinctively pacifist. It sought to end war by refusing to serve in time of war. The important change that occurred in the theory of the refusal to serve in war was the shift from individual, religious conscientious objection which never conceived of stopping or preventing war to war resistance which was a mass movement technique that sought to abolish war by enlisting large numbers of people who would refuse to cooperate with it.

Page's outline for peace in 1934 in no way summed up the whole of his own thought on peace or that of his comrades; the pacifists examined and adopted every idea that they could weave into the fabric of their program without destroying its inner symmetry. The attempt to create peace by removing the causes of war meant that a good share of pacifist thought was negative in its approach. This was true, in a vivid way, in the fight waged against militarism—a fight that even produced a bit of humor in the writing of the usually sedate pacifists. They battled militarism because they saw in it the perpetuation of the idea that war was inevitable, the idea that armaments bring security, the accentuating of nationalism, the belittling of the importance and effectiveness of international agencies, the creation of fear and tension among nations, and the expenditure of vast sums of money that could have been used for domestic social and economic reforms. Villard gave vent to the despair that ths endless reliance on preparedness brought to him: ". . . the dance of death is on. The world must arm, and arm, and arm. Who really cares what will happen?"[83]

The pacifists moved to the attack by scattering their shot at every indication of militarism. This ranged from the sale of military toys to army and navy appropriations. Of military toys they said, "You can get everything you want, from tanks to submarines, to tickle Junior's imagination and give him a killer's thrill."[84] They repeated with satisfaction that Winston Churchill had admitted that the 1,500 toy soldiers he had played with as a child had determined his life's course.[85] The

[82] Devere Allen, "War Resistance Old and New," *The World Tomorrow,* XIV (November, 1931), 364.

[83] Oswald Garrison Villard, "Gentlemen May Cry Peace," *The Saturday Review of Literature,* XI (April 6, 1935), 607.

[84] *The World Tomorrow,* XIV (February, 1931), 36.

[85] *Ibid.,* 37.

fight on military preparedness was a much more serious matter. The only weapons the pacifists possessed, for the most part, were those of education and publicity. Periodicals such as *The Nation, The Christian Century* and *The World Tomorrow* printed dozens of articles and editorials, and amassed column upon column of statistics and factual data, charting the course of armaments and their costs in every nation, the movements and pronouncements of military officials, and the actions and profits of business, industry, and the munitions interests in their pursuit of government contracts. Allen linked the preparedness program and the development of terrifying weapons of war with the growth of the militaristic control of industry, science, and government. George Coe saw in the Civilian Military Training Corps evidence of the deliberate extension of militaristic control over the thinking of the citizenry.[86]

The pacifists fought every appropriation for the army, navy, and veterans with their weapon of words and, on occasion, with some political pressure. Ernest Meyer, an embittered veteran of the corps of conscientious objectors imprisoned at Fort Leavenworth during the First World War, suggested to the pacifists that it was foolish to fight the American Legion. Far better to encourage and aid them, he showed, for their continuing "raids" on the United States Treasury were the surest way to drive the public into the pacifist ranks.[87] Experience, however, also bred cynicism "The trouble with the liberal press is that it supposes the American public is being led into the pacifist camp by philosophical speculations on the uselessness of war. . . . Nothing can be more erroneous. The American public rarely speculates, save on the stock exchange."[88] One instance of effective pacifist political pressure was the Nye committee hearings on the munitions industry in 1935, the inspiration for which the pacifist lobbyist, Dorothy Detzer, has been given the credit.[89] A clever device of publicizing the battle against militarism was developed by the Women's International League for Peace and Freedom. It consisted of a sticker to be pasted on the federal income tax return carrying the legend: "That part of this income which is levied for preparation for war is paid only under protest."[90] In 1940 Villard suggested having the leaders of all national parties in the country sign a joint declaration that there would never again be conscription in the United States.[91] Needless to say these proved

[86] George Albert Coe, "Training Citizens—For What?" *The World Tomorrow,* IX (October, 1926), 151-154.

[87] Ernest L. Meyer, "A Pacifist Defends the Legion," *The Christian Century,* XLIX (November 9, 1932), 1373.

[88] *Ibid.,* 1373.

[89] John W. Masland, "Pressure Groups and American Foreign Policy," *The Public Opinion Quarterly,* VI (Spring, 1942), 115.

[90] *The World Tomorrow,* XV (April, 1932), 116.

[91] Oswald Garrison Villard, "Issues and Men," *The Nation,* CXLVIII (April 15, 1939), 432.

to be futile gestures, powerless to combat effectively the forces of the preparedness movement.

No single aspect of the military picture received more attention from the pacifists than the Reserve Officers Training Corps established under the National Defense Act of 1920. The extent of the pacifists' interest in this invasion of the universities, colleges, and high schools was well illustrated in H. C. Engelbrecht's article "The Camel and the Arab" in *The World Tomorrow* for February, 1929. Engelbrecht presented a documented study of the influence of military instruction in the curricula of colleges and universities by analyzing such factors as credit points, growth in the number of courses, relative emphasis given in college catalogues, the statements about the value of such training, and its influence on the school libraries.[92] This picture of the penetration of militarism into the traditional activities and practices of the academic world was not a cheery one, nor was Reinhold Niebuhr's charge in 1926 that the R.O.T.C., whether consciously or unconsciously, was developing not simply military skills, but a "military mentality" as well.[93] Even the Boy Scouts could not escape the scrutiny of the pacifists who saw in their drill, discipline, uniform, and their sham battles evidences of the corroding work of militarism.[94]

The church, too, was taken to task over the services of its pastors in the chaplain corps during the war. This pacifist protest against ministers serving in the army can be traced back a hundred years; it was revived again in the inter-war period. The reason, as Page explained it, was that the ". . . military chaplain is an official part of the army, wears an army uniform, receives his salary from the war department, and must obey orders of his superior officers."[95] Some pacifists proposed that ministers should serve the men in the armed forces in an un-official capacity receiving pay from their churches. Kirby Page went so far as to suggest that candidates for the ministry who showed a willingness to participate in or sanction war should be denied ordination.[96] In a poll conducted in 1934, he received the statements of 8,014 clergymen who said that they could not conscientiously serve as chaplains.[97] In this variety of ways the pacifists hunted out and exposed the evidences of the military wherever they found them in American life.

[92] H. C. Engelbrecht, "The Camel and the Arab," *The World Tomorrow,* XII (February, 1929), 58-60.

[93] Reinhold Niebuhr, "The Threat of the R.O.T.C.," *The World Tomorrow,* IX (October, 1926), 154.

[94] *The World Tomorrow,* XIII (June, 1930), 246-247.

[95] Kirby Page, "If War Is Sin," *The Christian Century,* LII (January 9, 1934), 44.

[96] *Ibid.,* p. 44.

[97] Kirby Page, "20,870 Clergymen on War and Economic Injustice," *The World Tomorrow,* XVII (May 10, 1934), 226.

Their efforts were directed most often at the obvious, and often superficial, manifestations of the militaristic spirit. To combat the slow penetration of this spirit into the thought of the people, posed a challenge to their imagination and insight which they seldom met.

Yet the pacifists did not entirely ignore the challenge of long-term transformation or redirection of human interests and institutions.[98] Education was of central concern in peace thinking. The pacifists agreed that peace was impossible until a revolution in thought and action had occurred within each individual. Despite the preoccupation with ideas of mass action of a non-violent nature and with the achievements of Gandhi in India, the pacifist remained individual-oriented. His reliance upon education as the key to the new world held firm; the pacifist's theory of human nature as essentially good and rational justified for him this abiding concern. Devere Allen believed that the intricate legalistic structure which he and other pacifists were so diligent in supporting could not be trusted in the last analysis because aggression was indefinable. The only sure hope of peace, he concluded, was an enlightened world public opinion motivated by the "will-to-peace."[99]

Pacifists spoke a great deal about creating "will-to-peace," "friendship," or the "international mind and heart." Harold Bosley witnessing the whole peace structure collapse before his eyes, wrote in 1938 that the only hope of the world was the ". . . creation of a radical peace sentiment. . . ."[100] Reacting to the superpatriotism of the early twenties, pacifists called for a new patriotism characterized by H. C. Engelbrecht as "intelligent and realistic" in that it sought out the important institutions, movements, and problems of the nation, "critical" in that it discriminated between the good and evil on the national scene, praising and supporting the former while opposing the latter, and "humanitarian" in that it encompassed with friendship the world in its outlook.[101] Page pictured a new concept of national honor that could be offended only by actions, never by words, and a change in the dogma of national sovereignty by the acceptance of a world-wide responsibility.[102] William Ladd, a century before, had called for the "weakening" of the chauvinistic sort of patriotism but found it always a dangerous thing at

[98] Kirby Page, "A New National Preparedness," *The Forum,* LXXXI (February, 1929), 73.

[99] Devere Allen, "The Slippery Aggressor," *The World Tomorrow,* XIII (June, 1930), 254-258.

[100] Harold Bosley, "A Defense of Radical Peace Sentiment," *The Christian Century,* LV (November 2, 1938), 1325.

[101] H. C. Engelbrecht, "Pacifism and Patriotism," *The World Tomorrow,* XI (July, 1928), 296-297.

[102] Kirby Page, "Overcoming Evil with Good in International Affairs," *The World Tomorrow,* IX (November, 1926), 214.

any time to hope to discuss patriotism and expect to be understood.[103] George Coe believed it essential to resist the sweep of "perverted" patriotism, to remember that the state was not the final moral authority and to rid the mind of old sentimental ideas about war and peace.[104]

Page considered that the goal of this education was to instill in the mind the fact that war was sin and that participation in war, far from being a matter of individual conscience, was illegitimate for the Christian. Young people "must" be taught, he believed, that they could not rightfully enroll in military training courses in school.[105] Coe put the desire of Page in psychological terms when he spoke of bringing the "actualities of war-making and peace-making" into the "mental foreground" and revealing once and for all the "deep-lying dynamics" of war-making.[106] He too believed that one object of peace education must be to teach the young to resist military training in school.[107] Georgia Harkness called for building resistance to war hysteria and totalitarian psychology.[108]

A. Hamilton Gibbs conceived of the goal of peace education in a more positive light as implanting in men's minds the idea that peace was inevitable. All gains in human civilization, he contended, have resulted from the sublimation of primal restraints such as greed, fear, and desire. The new outlook could be rooted in another primal instinct—that of gregariousness. Peace was possible thus when men saw in it the fulfillment of their desires for friendship and fellowship.[109]

When pacifists turned from the statement of goals to the problem of how to inculcate the values desired, they often defined the method simply as "education," or "slow reeducation," or "an educational campaign," as if the words themselves were magic keys that disclosed all mysteries and solved all difficulties. A few essayed the more difficult but necessary venture of describing the method to be used. Coe described the task as "shifting the national mind-set" for which he could prescribe two procedures. The first was to teach what he termed "objective" history; he was quite sure such a thing existed, and assorted confidently: "War thrives upon misunderstandings, half-truths, preju-

[103] Devere Allen, *The Fight for Peace* (New York: The Macmillan Company, 1930), p. 232. (Hereinafter cited as Allen, *Fight for Peace.*)

[104] George Albert Coe, "Educating for Peace and Not for War," *The World Tomorrow,* XIV (November, 1931), 360.

[105] Kirby Page, "If War Is Sin," *The Christian Century,* LII (January 9, 1935), 43-44.

[106] George Albert Coe, "Educating for Peace and Not for War," *The World Tomorrow,* XIV (November, 1931), 360.

[107] *Ibid.,* p. 361.

[108] Georgia Harkness, "Are Pacifists Romantics?" *The Christian Century,* LV (June 1, 1928), 694.

[109] A. Hamilton Gibbs, "Moral Preparedness for the Next War," *The Survey,* LVII (April 1, 1927), 10-13.

dices. The cause of peace is naturally affiliated with the objectivity of the scientific and historic spirit."[110] The pursuit of this method meant a vigilant fight against the "dogmatic militarism" superpatriotic groups were attempting to write into history textbooks and the replacing of such militarism, not by a "dogmatic pacifism" but by the presentation of data in their "naked objectivity."

The second course of action was the development of a "discriminating" patriotism by which Coe meant the awareness whenever one performed a patriotic act, such as saluting the flag, of precisely what aspects of the national life you were paying tribute to and, therefore, also the awareness of those aspects for which improvement or change were to be sought. The key to this process was the attitude of the educator which must first be changed before peace would be possible for the public.[111] Paul Jones saw that man's basic need of fellowship made possible a road to peace by bringing men together; he wrote: "It is possible to bring groups of people into contact with the result that the contact merely provides occasion for new outbursts of antagonism and prejudice. Where, however, such people who have different ideas, different prejudices, and different ways of doing things, can be led into some kind of genuine cooperation, a process is thereupon set in motion by which prejudices and antagonisms tend to fall away."[112] To Jones the character of man was not fixed, but flexible and plastic.

There was as well a medley of suggested techniques: the description of the aims and effects of conscription, the revelation of the truth about the First World War, the circulation of peace literature,[113] and the training of religious leaders to be experts in leading discussions.[114] Holmes thought it would be sufficient if each individual would devote himself to some program or movement, it mattered little which one, that sought the abolition of war.[115] Mrs. Carrie Catt believed that if only people were taught to "think straight" these programs and their leaders would automatically emerge.[116]

The desire for peace through education did not remain entirely an intellectual plaything. It was translated into several concrete activities

[110] George Albert Coe, "Shifting the National Mind-Set," *The World Tomorrow,* VII (February, 1924), 42.

[111] *Ibid.,* 42-43.

[112] Paul Jones, "The Enigma of Fellowship," *The World Tomorrow,* XIII (August, 1930), 327-328.

[113] Kirby Page, "A Program for Peace Action," *The Christian Century,* LII (May 15, 1935), 635.

[114] George Albert Coe, "Shifting the National Mind-Set," *The World Tomorrow,* VII (February, 1924), 43.

[115] John Haynes Holmes, "What Anyone Can Do," *The World Tomorrow,* VII (February, 1924), 56.

[116] Carrie Chapman Catt, "Can the Church Stop War?" *The World Tomorrow,* XIV (June, 1931), 189.

by pacifists, despite their limited resources. Devere Allen, for example, founded the Nofrontier News Service in 1933 with the aid of Ray Newton, secretary of the Peace Section of the American Friends Service Committee. The Nofrontier News Service provided professional news bulletins, editorials, articles on the cause of peace and pacifism for the religious, labor, rural, and the small city press throughout the United States.[117] A similar attempt to bring peace to the attention of the public was the World Peaceways program of advertising peace through the media of billboards, posters, movies, magazines, and even a radio news broadcast. In 1930 this organization staged an automobile caravan that toured the United States bearing the "Biggest Book in the World" upon the pages of which over a million people signed a petition for a peace department.[118]

The idea of a peace department in the government, first proposed by Dr. Benjamin Rush in 1790, was given its fullest treatment in the inter-war period by Kirby Page.[119] With elaborate detail Page demonstrated what a department with a budget of $100,000,000—one-sixth of the expenses of the army and the navy for 1929—could do for the cause of peace. Included in the budget besides the administrative expenses of the secretary, his staff, and of the ten regional and forty foreign offices envisaged, were provisions for the free circulation of millions of booklets and books, the production of movies, an extensive student and faculty exchange program with foreign nations, a peace scholarship program, summer camp expenses for forty thousand young people, World Fellowship cruises, and the erection of peace monuments.[120] Page's ideas never advanced beyond the dream stage, nor did they provoke much serious discussion among the pacifists, though an organization—the American Association for World Peace—was formed in Atascadero, California, in 1926 for the express purpose of campaigning for legislation creating such a department.[121]

The pacifists in their ambition to win the peace through education and propaganda showed an unwarranted reliance upon literary persuasion which deterred them from developing political and economic techniques of writing into law the items of their peace program. There was, indeed, an inherent difficulty never overcome in making peace

[117] Devere Allen, "News for Peace," *The World Tomorrow,* XVI (October 26, 1933), 595-596.

[118] Theresa Mayer Durlach, "A Plan for Mass Education," *The World Tomorrow,* XVI (December 7, 1933), 667; Merle Curti, *Peace or War: The American Struggle 1636-1936* (New York: W. W. Norton and Company, 1936), pp. 274-275.

[119] Allen, *Fight for Peace,* p. 245.

[120] Kirby Page, "A New National Preparedness," *The Forum,* LXXXI (February, 1929), 73.

[121] Allen, *Fight for Peace,* p. 248.

education and propaganda attractive and compelling; the glamor and excitement of war continued to maintain its hold on American life and thought.

Other methods than education were not ignored, but, like the discussion of education, the ideas proposed were rarely translated into any form of meaningful activity. Norman Thomas talked in terms of a general strike against war, a political-propagandist device.[122] Devere Allen visualized a strike combining the forces of the clergy, labor, teachers, and other groups against war.[123] One political technique that did win wide support and reached the halls of Congress in the form of a proposed constitutional amendment called for a popular referendum on war. Here again was another instance of the negative orientation of so much of pacifist thought. The idea was not new; Bryan and the Populists had advocated it long before the First World War. Nor was it distinctly pacifist; it graced the platform of the La Follette Conference for Progressive Political Action in 1924. Essentially it was a progressive concept which found strong support in pacifist circles. A Duluth, Minnesota medical doctor, Thomas Hall Shastid, was responsible for leading a nation-wide campaign to legislate the referendum.[124] The projected amendment prohibited gifts and loans for war purposes to foreign nations and provided that Congress could not declare a war without submitting the question to a vote of the American people.[125] Villard was the outspoken advocate of the referendum; writing in 1935, for example, he said: ". . . war has now become such a monstrous thing, so diabolical in all its aspects, and so certain, as we all now know, to ruin victors and vanquished alike, that no one man, no small group of men, no Congress shall have the right to declare war."[126] The assumption in pacifist thinking that the American people would never vote to go to war was strangely at variance with the pacifist's educational program. The latter assumed that the "national mind-set" needed to be transformed and that the public must be educated in the ways of peace. Sayre spoke as well of a "propaganda of truth" campaign as a psychological device for winning the peace.[127] Page, sensing the need for color and drama, suggested the use of mass demonstrations and

[122] Norman Thomas, "Is Peaceful Revolution Possible?" *The World Tomorrow,* XV (September 14, 1932), 253.

[123] Devere Allen, "Pacifism in the World Crisis," *The World Tomorrow,* XIV (December, 1931), 394.

[124] Thomas Hall Shastid, "The War-Check Vote," *The World Tomorrow,* XII (March, 1929), 120-122.

[125] *Ibid.,* 120.

[126] Oswald Garrison Villard, "If This Be Treason," *The Nation,* CXLI (October 9, 1935), 399.

[127] John Nevin Sayre, "Pacifism and National Security," *The World Tomorrow,* XI (August, 1928), 333.

parades with posters, placards, and displays against armed preparedness, the R.O.T.C., or in support of the League of Nations.[128]

The pacifists were sensitive to the need of making peace an appealing idea to the people. They talked about staging plays, pageants, and dance-dramas, and designing an "aesthetic" program that would help create the new mind-set they desired; ". . . let the rhythms of industry and labor, of religion and freedom have colorful presentation," wrote William Bridge.[129] John Haynes Holmes contributed a pacifist play "If This Be Treason" to a growing list of anti-war and peace plays including works by Maxwell Anderson and Lawrence Stallings ("What Price Glory?"), Sidney Howard ("Paths of Glory"), W. Somerset Maugham ("For Services Rendered"), Paul Green ("Johnny Johnson"), Robert Sherwood ("Idiot's Delight"), and Irwin Shaw ("Bury the Dead").[130] Benjamin Musser called for poets to arise in every land to speak peace.[131] E. Merrill Root eloquently intoned a chant for the "wine of poetry" and the "bread of prose" that would ". . . make art and philosophy magic casements opening on the foam of perilous seas in faerylands that are not forlorn."[132] Unfortunately Root's vision failed to stir the genius of artists who would create the lovely world for which he longed. William Bridge, in all-too-familiar terms, proposed a general conference of peace workers with artists who were interested in world understanding which would provide the incentive needed.[133] Sayre too voiced the need of some sort of international organization of artists.[134] One small note of encouragement came in Gladys Meyerand's description of cultural projects being carried on in the settlement houses in New York City. Pageants, plays, folklore, drama, an international orchestra, decorating rooms in the modes of the different nationalities represented in the settlement, games, individual art projects, and handicrafts had been used successfully to create the understanding contacts and a friendly environment between peoples of diverse cultures that Paul Jones considered to be the way to peace.[135]

[128] Kirby Page, "A Program for Peace Action," *The Christian Century,* LII (May 15, 1935), 635-636.

[129] William H. Bridge to the Editors of *The World Tomorrow, The World Tomorrow,* XIV (September, 1931), 301.

[130] Karl M. Chworowsky, "The Drama Against War," *The Christian Century,* LVII (February 28, 1940), 278-281.

[131] Benjamin Francis Musser, "On Poetry and War," *The Catholic World,* CXXXIX (September, 1934), 703.

[132] E. Merrill Root, "Life's Bread and Wine," *The World Tomorrow,* IX (March, 1926), 73.

[133] William H. Bridge to the Editors of *The World Tomorrow, The World Tomorrow,* XIV (September, 1931), 301.

[134] John Nevin Sayre, "Disarmament and Defense," *The World Tomorrow,* V (January, 1922), 4.

[135] Gladys E. Meyerand, "Art and the Peace Crusade," *The World Tomorrow,* XIII (September, 1930), 371-373.

The agency the pacifists looked to above all others to bring this change in human thought and action was the church. A deep undercurrent of feeling that the church was responsible for peace permeated pacifist thought. There was a sense of guilt about its failure to halt war and its support of war in the course of nineteen hundred years. If the church failed again, many said, it would have to bear the responsibility for the destruction and accept the condemnation of mankind.

The pacifists perceived in an awakened church their finest hope for leadership toward a just and durable peace. Every resolution by an official church body, every pacifist stand taken by a minister or rabbi was felt as another blow at the war system. The hope did not die easily; in the face of another holocaust that would envelop Europe in a few short months pacifists still looked toward the church: ". . . we call upon the church to enter into deeper fellowship with that church which refused to serve in Caesar's armies, and to invite into its unbreakable spiritual community the men and women of all lands who pray night and day for peace."[136] Some who were more sensitive to the reality of the situation knew that there was no earthly institution such as the "church" but only many churches; that there were no indications that the congregations or people were supporting the churches in their denunciation of war; or that the masses of the unchurched were flocking to the churches that took such a stand.[137] In these circumstances a few directed their attention to the creation of cells of pacifist Christians within the church to perform their mission as a leavening agent. The party organization of the Communists throughout the Western world furnished a lucid example of the power such a group could exert. Kagawa had adopted this method among Christians in Japan. A. J. Muste spoke of this church within the church as the "true international" picturing to himself a militant dynamic force like Lenin's party system.[138] H. Richard Niebuhr proposed that groups be formed of nonresistants who ". . . divorcing themselves from the program of nationalism and of capitalism, unite in a higher loyalty which transcends national and class lines of division and prepare for the future."[139] The activity of these cells would be that of purging themselves of self-righteousness through self-analysis in anticipation of the day when the deterministic social processes would have brought to pass the Kingdom. Resembling the Communists in organization, they differed dramatically

[136] "Christian Pacifists Take Their Stand," *The Christian Century,* LVI (March 15, 1939), 345.

[137] Frederick Lynch, "War and the Churches," *The World Tomorrow,* XII (June, 1929), 274-275.

[138] A. J. Muste, "The True International," *The Christian Century,* XLIX (March 23, 1932), 379.

[139] Helmut Richard Niebuhr, "The Grace of Doing Nothing," *The Christian Century,* XLIV (March 23, 1932), 379.

in purpose and action. Cadoux desired a similar inner-group but not one divorced from society. Resembling the religious orders of the Catholic church, it would be a band of nonresistant pacifists expressing in the tasks of service and love the meaning of their faith.[140] Sayre suggested a "shock" battalion of unarmed soldiers who would go anywhere in the world where there were hostilities or threats of hostility and would "absorb evil" and forgive all.[141]

Pacifists called for a reuniting of the churches, for a joint declaration of all churches denouncing war. Rufus Jones was sure that if only the example of the American Friends Service Committee with the work of love and service in areas of war and hate could be expanded to include all churches, war would cease.[142] Christian pacifists knew that love, service, and sacrifice were the only true weapons by which the day of peace would become a reality; these qualities were in fact the distinguishing characteristics of the peace they desired.

But pacifist plans for the role of the church did not move beyond the realm of talk. This failure in relationship to the church—the one institution with which most pacifists were intimately related and thus the institution through which they could have been expected to work out the realization of their plans—indicated a lack of organizational leadership and necessary human and monetary resources. It also reflected the fact that pacifism did not become a "cause" in the inter-war period, but remained an idea or faith attached to other faiths. It became in various hands a subdivision of socialism, of social religion, or of the radical labor movement. Men who called themselves pacifists were only partly so; they were primarily ministers, labor leaders, educators, or journalists. Pacifism in the inter-war period lacked a leader of the stature of Elihu Burritt or William Ladd who would devote his life to pacifism alone and give practical, organized expression to the fertile thought that characterized the pacifist movement.

The nature of the peace sought remained largely undefined by the pacifists. Peace was a most elusive concept and the pacifists avoided defining it either because they assumed a general understanding of its nature or because they realized the difficulty of attempting to verbalize a desire or feeling. It would seem that for most, peace meant a world without war, a world where disputes among nations were settled peace-

[140] C. J. Cadoux, "The Christian Pacifist Case," *The Journal of Religion,* XXI (July, 1941), 241.

[141] John Nevin Sayre, "War Is Unchristian, But—," *The World Tomorrow,* VII (February, 1924), 54.

[142] Rufus Matthew Jones, "A Great 'Experiment'," *Survey Graphic,* XXXI (August, 1942), 355.

fully.[143] The pacifists' touchiness about the negative aspect of his ideas would dispose them to the latter phrasing. It was this definition of peace implicit in their thought that largely determined the nature of their thinking about the ways of bringing peace to the world. A second, and essentially positive, assumption of the nature of peace permeated the thought of the pacifists of this period as a result of the union of pacifism with the social gospel and socialism. Thus peace became synonymous with a better social order or the coming of the Kingdom. Thomas saw peace as a commonwealth of socialist nations.[144] Page, adopting this to the phraseology of social religion, saw peace as a society organized and operated on principles of love and persuasion.[145] Page spoke as well of a transformed economic order and a cooperative social system.[146] This was true of the social gospel pacifists; their identification of peace with the social gospel produced the tension we have noted and vigorously expanded the content and scope of their thought. A few bravely attempted to give expression to the spirit or feeling of peace. Lewisohn termed it the "resistless love of life."[147] Smucker thought it meant an association of virtues: justice, healthy people, a robust culture, general security.[148] "Peace," Elihu Burritt had said a century ago, "is a spirit, and not an intellectual abstraction; it is a life, not a theory."[149] When pacifism moved from the realm of abstract slogan and thought and became embodied in a living personality, it created the sort of life men have called good. Muste realized this central truth when he said that ". . . peace is a seamless garment that must cover the whole of life and must be applied in all its relationships."[150]

The most potent challenge to peace and pacifism during the inter-war period, however, was the press of circumstances. In a real sense there was no meeting of minds between the pacifist and non-pacifist. The one argued in terms of ideals, of absolute principles of eternal value; the other argued in terms of the demands of the day. To many from 1931 on, pacifism seemed to be a most dangerous faith because it

[143] Kirby Page, "A New National Preparedness," *The Forum,* LXXXI (February, 1929), 74.

[144] Norman Thomas, "Removing Economic Barriers to Peace," *The World Tomorrow,* XIV (November, 1931), 358.

[145] Kirby Page, "But Evil Must Be Conquered," *The World Tomorrow,* IX (October, 1926), 169.

[146] Kirby Page, "International Economic Cooperation," *The World Tomorrow,* XII (September, 1929), 371.

[147] Ludwig Lewisohn, "Levy Versus Smith," *The Saturday Review of Literature,* V (March 9, 1929), 753.

[148] Donovan E. Smucker to the Editor of *The Nation, The Nation,* CXLIX (September 16, 1939), 303.

[149] Allen, *Fight for Peace,* p. 420.

[150] A. J. Muste, "Return to Pacifism," *The Christian Century,* LIII (December 2, 1936), 1605.

threatened to leave the nation defenseless in the path of the irrational power of the totalitarian states. It is impossible to measure the effect of pacifism in preventing the United States from having a positive foreign policy backed by armaments sufficient to be commensurate with our position in world affairs. If this contention were true then the pacifists must be credited with the remarkable feat of influencing millions. But this would be a gross misreading of public apathy, indifference or weariness, as a conscious response to the pacifist message. The one dangerous aspect of pacifist thought from 1935 on was that it provided an idealistic rationalization for those who by nature were disposed to isolationism.

Isolationism and pacifism were uncomfortable partners in the period from the attack on Manchuria in 1931 to Pearl Harbor. By the mid-thirties the pacifists, believing ". . . that war abroad could no longer be prevented and that America must therefore insulate herself . . .,"[151] joined in support of the policies and actions that would keep the United States out of war. The pacifists took this stance because they had defined war as the absolute evil. They fought for all the neutrality legislation with the tightest possible restrictions. They fought the transfer of the fifty destroyers, the conception of the United States as an arsenal of democracy, the lend-lease law, conscription, the lifting of the ban on sending troops out of this hemisphere, and the repeal of the neutrality law.[152] Until 1940 pacifists were the leaders of the "neutrality bloc" program of lobbying and propagandizing in Washington.[153] That they were uncomfortable should be obvious from this description of their companions in the battle: ". . . shoulder to shoulder, stand the Chicago *Tribune,* and the *Daily Worker,* the United States Chamber of Commerce and the American Youth Congress, the National Economy League and the Women's International League for Peace and Freedom, Mrs. Albert Dilling and Robert M. Hutchins, Father Coughlin and the La Follettes."[154] Pacifist leadership in the fight, concentrated in the Keep America Out of War Congress, gave way to the isolationist forces represented by the creation of the No Foreign War Committee and the America First Committee in 1940. Pacifists were deeply suspicious of these groups and cooperated little with them directly. Two organizations

[151] John W. Masland, "Pressure Groups and American Foreign Policy," *The Public Opinion Quarterly,* VI (Spring, 1942), 116.

[152] *The Christian Century,* LIX (February 11, 1942), 188.

[153] John W. Masland, "Pressure Groups and American Foreign Policy," *The Public Opinion Quarterly,* VI (Spring, 1942), 116.

[154] Stanley High, "The Liberals' War," *The Nation,* CLII (June 14, 1941), 691.

formed in 1941, the Ministers' No War Committee and the Churchmen's Campaign for Peace and Mediation, received pacifist support.[155]

Their discomfort came in larger measure from their critics who pointed out in mercilessly clear language the barbarities and cruelties of the fascist forces and the threat they posed to all of civilization, for the pacifists sought not only peace but social justice and the end to oppression. Once again the full force of the tension inherent in modern pacifism became apparent. Once again war dashed the hopes of peace lovers.

[155] Florence R. Flourney, "The Protestant Churches and the War," *The South Atlantic Quarterly,* XLII (April, 1943), 116.

BIBLIOGRAPHY

BIBLIOGRAPHY

Primary Materials

As is evident from the text and footnotes, this study is largely built upon information and opinion derived from contemporary periodicals. Issues of the following publications were thoroughly combed for the entire interwar period: *The Christian Century*, *The World Tomorrow*, *The Nation*, and *The New Republic*. Where items relevant to the themes explored in the volume appeared in the following journals they were also examined: *The Atlantic Monthly*, *The American Mercury*, *The Catholic World*, *The Commonweal*, *The Forum*, *Harper's Monthly*, *The Living Age*, *National Republic*, *The Outlook*, *The Saturday Review of Literature*, *The Survey*, and *Survey Graphic*.

Secondary Books and Articles

Allen, Devere. *The Fight for Peace*. New York: The Macmillan Company, 1930.

———. "The Peace Movement Moves Left," *The Annals* of the American Academy of Political and Social Science, CLXXV (September, 1934), 150-155.

Angell, Norman. "Current Criticisms of the Peace Front," in *Geneva and the Drift to War*. ("Problems Of Peace." Twelfth Series.) (London: George Allen and Unwin, 1938), 198-207.

———. "Pacifism," in *Encyclopaedia of the Social Sciences*. 15 volumes. Edited by Edwin R. A. Seligman and Alvin Johnson. (New York: The Macmillan Company, 1930-1935), XI, 527-528.

Beales, A. C. F. *The History of Peace: A Short Account of the Organized Movements for International Peace*. New York: The Dial Press, 1931.

Beloff, Max. "Historians in a Revolutionary Age," *Foreign Affairs*, XXIX (January, 1951), 248-262.

Bogart, Ernest Ludlow. *Direct and Indirect Causes of the Great World War*. (Number 24, Edward Kinley, ed., "Preliminary Economic Studies of the War." Carnegie Endowment for International Peace.) New York: Oxford University Press, 1919.

Cadoux, C. J. "The Christian Pacifist Case," *The Journal of Religion*, XXI (July, 1941), 233-242.

Catholic Authors: Contemporary Biographical Sketches 1930-1947. Edited by Matthew Hoehn. Newark: St. Mary's Abbey, 1948.

Chase, Don M. "What Sort of People Are Pacifists?" *The World Tomorrow,* XII (February, 1929), 83-84.

Childs, Harwood L. "Public Opinion and Peace," *The Annals* of the American Academy of Political and Social Science, CXCII (July, 1937), 31-37.

Chworowsky, Karl M. "The Drama Against War," *The Christian Century,* LVII (February 28, 1940), 278-281.

Curti, Merle. *The Growth of American Thought.* New York: Harper and Brothers, 1943.

———. *Peace or War: The American Struggle 1636-1936.* New York: W. W. Norton and Company, 1936.

Davies, D. R. *Reinhold Niebuhr: Prophet from America.* New York: The Macmillan Company, 1948.

Drake, J. G. St. Clair. "Who Are Jehovah's Witnesses?" *The Christian Century,* LIII (April 15, 1936), 567-570.

Droba, D. D. "Effect of Various Factors on Militarism-Pacifism," *The Journal of Abnormal and Social Psychology,* XXVI (July-September, 1931), 141-153.

Earle, Edward Mead. "A Half-Century of American Foreign Policy," *Political Science Quarterly,* LXIV (June, 1949), 168-188.

Eddy, Sherwood. *Eighty Adventurous Years: An Autobiography.* New York: Harper and Brothers, 1955.

Ellis, L. Ethan. *Frank B. Kellogg and American Foreign Relations, 1925-1929.* New Brunswick: Rutgers University Press, 1961.

Ferrell, Robert H. *Peace in Their Time: The Origins of the Kellogg-Briand Pact.* New Haven: Yale University Press, 1952.

———. "The Peace Movement," in *Isolation and Security.* Edited by Alexander DeConde. (Durham, N. C., Duke University Press, 1957), 82-106.

Field, G. C. *Pacifism and Conscientious Objection.* Cambridge, England: Cambridge University Press, 1945.

Flournoy, Florence R. "The Protestant Churches and the War," *The South Atlantic Quarterly,* XLII (April, 1943), 113-125.

Friedrich, Carl Joachim. *Inevitable Peace.* Cambridge: Harvard University Press, 1948.

Gabriel, Ralph Henry. *The Course of American Democratic Thought: An Intellectual History Since 1815.* New York: The Ronald Press, 1940.

Gregg, Richard B. *The Power of Nonviolence.* Second Revised Edition. Nyack, New York: Fellowship Publications, 1959.

Gundlach, Ralph H. "The Changing Policies of Peace and Patriotic

Societies," *The Journal of Social Psychology*, XV (February, 1942), 192-195.

Hartmann, George W. "Motivational Differences Between Pacifists and Non-Pacifists," *The Journal of Social Psychology*, XIV (August, 1941), 197-210.

———. "The Strength and Weakness of the Pacifist Position As Seen by American Philosophers," *The Philosophical Review*, LIII (March, 1944), 125-144.

Hershberger, Guy Franklin. *War, Peace, and Nonresistance*. Scottdale, Pennsylvania: The Herald Press, 1946.

Holloway, Vernon H. "A Review of American Religious Pacifism," *Religion in Life*, XIX (Summer, 1950), 367-379.

Hopkins, Charles Howard. *The Rise of the Social Gospel in American Protestantism 1865-1915*. New Haven: Yale University Press, 1940.

Howe, Irving and Lewis Coser. *The American Communist Party: A Critical History*. Second Edition. New York: Frederick A. Praeger, 1962.

Hudson, Manley O. "Postwar Progress Toward World Peace," *The Annals* of the American Academy of Political and Social Science, CLXXIV (July, 1934), 141-149.

Hughley, J. Neal. *Trends in Protestant Social Idealism*. Morningside Heights, New York: King's Crown Press, 1948.

Huxley, Aldous Leonard. *An Encyclopaedia of Pacifism*. New York: Harper and Brothers, 1937.

Johnson, Alvin. "War," in *Encyclopaedia of the Social Sciences*. 15 volumes. Edited by Edwin R. A. Seligman and Alvin Johnson. (New York: The Macmillan Company, 1930-1935), XV, 331-342.

Jones, Rufus Matthew. *The Faith and Practice of the Quakers*. Seventh Edition. London: Methuen and Company, 1949.

Knox, John. "Re-examining Pacifism," in *Religion and the Present Crisis*. (Chicago: University of Chicago Press, 1942), 30-47.

Lee, Umphrey. *The Historic Church and Modern Pacifism*. New York: Abingdon-Cokesbury Press, 1943.

Leopold, Richard W. "The Problem of American Intervention, 1917: An Historical Retrospect," *World Politics*, II (April, 1950), 405-425.

Libby, Frederick J. "The Problem of Peace," in *Beyond Dilemmas: Quakers Look at Life*. Edited by J. B. Laughlin. (New York: J. B. Lippincott Company, 1937), 284-292.

Lincoln, Abraham. *The Collected Works of Abraham Lincoln*. 8 volumes. Edited by Roy P. Basler. New Burnswick: Rutgers University Press, 1953.

Link, Arthur Stanley. *American Epoch: A History of the United States Since the 1890's.* New York: Alfred A. Knopf, 1955.

Lovett, Robert Morss. *Jane Addams and the Women's International League for Peace and Freedom.* Chicago: Chicago Branch of the National Jane Addams Peace Fund Committee, 1946.

McConnell, Francis J. "The Churches and the War Problem," *The Annals* of the American Academy of Political and Social Science, CLXXV (September, 1934), 143-149.

Maddox, William P. "Is American Labor Pacifist?" *The American Scholar,* IV (Winter, 1935), 86-97.

Martin, David A. *Pacifism: An Historical and Sociological Study.* New York: Schocken Books, 1966.

Maslund, John W. "Pressure Groups and American Foreign Policy," *The Public Opinion Quarterly,* VI (Spring, 1942), 115-122.

Neblett, Thomas F. "Youth Movements in the United States," *The Annals* of the American Academy of Political and Social Science, CXCIV (November, 1937), 141-151.

Nickerson, Hoffman. "The Tragic Failure of Pacifism," *The North American Review,* CCXLII (Autumn, 1936), 132-142.

Nixon, Justin Wroe. "A Nonpacifist Looks at Pacifism," *The Journal of Religion,* XXI (July, 1941), 243-252.

Peace Year Book 1933. London: National Peace Conference, 1933.

Plater, Charles. *A Primer of Peace and War: The Principles of International Morality.* New York: P. J. Kennedy and Sons, 1915.

Report of the Third Conference on the Cause and Cure of War: Held in Washington, D. C. January 15-19, 1928. Washington: n.p., 1928.

Riesman, David. "Some Observations on the Limits of Totalitarian Power," *The Antioch Review,* XII (June, 1952), 155-168.

Robinson, Henry Morton. *Fantastic Interim: A Hindsight History of American Manners, Morals, and Mistakes Between Versailles and Pearl Harbor.* New York: Harcourt, Brace and Company, 1943.

Seidman, Harold. "How Radical Are College Students?" *The American Scholar,* IV (Summer, 1935), 326-330.

Shannon, David A. *The Socialist Party of America.* New York: The Macmillan Company, 1955.

Sibley, Mulford Q. and Philip E. Jacob. *Conscription of Conscience: The American State and the Conscientious Objector, 1940-1947.* Ithaca: Cornell University Press, 1952.

Simonds, Frank H. "The Collapse of the Peace Movement," *The*

Annals of the American Academy of Political and Social Science, CLXXIV (July, 1934), 116-120.

Slosson, Preston William. *The Great Crusade and After 1914-1928.* (volume XII, Arthur Meier Schlesinger and Dixon Ryan Fox, eds., *A History of American Life.*) New York: The Macmillan Company, 1930.

Stevenson, Robert C. "The Evolution of Pacifism," *The International Journal of Ethics,* XLIV (July, 1934), 437-451.

Subject Headings Used in the Dictionary Catalogues of the Library of Congress. Fifth Edition. Edited by Nella Jane Martin. Washington: Library of Congress, 1948.

Van Kirk, Walter W. *Religion Renounces War.* Chicago: Willett, Clark and Company, 1934.

Villard, Oswald Garrison. *Fighting Years: Memoirs of a Liberal Editor.* New York: Harcourt, Brace and Company, 1939.

Wecter, Dixon. *The Age of the Great Depression 1929-1941.* (volume XIII, Arthur Meier Schlesinger and Dixon Ryan Fox, eds., *A History of American Life.*) New York: The Macmillan Company, 1948.

Weiss, Paul. "The Ethics of Pacifism," *The Philosophical Review,* LI (September, 1942), 476-496.

Wells, Frederic Lyman. "The Instinctive Bases of Pacifism," *The Atlantic Monthly,* CXVIII (July, 1916), 44-46.

Wilson, Woodrow. *President Wilson's State Papers and Addresses.* Edited by Albert Shaw. New York: George H. Doran Company, 1918.

Wood, James Playsted. *Magazines in the United States: Their Social and Economic Influence.* New York: The Ronald Press Company, 1949.

Woodman, Charles M. *Quakers Find a Way: Their Discoveries in Practical Living.* Indianapolis: The Bobbs-Merrill Company, 1950.

Wright, C. J. "The War and Human History or Scepticism and 'Pacifism'," *The London Quarterly and Holborn Review,* CLXVIII (April, 1943), 97-103.

Wright, Quincy. *A Study of War.* 2 volumes. Chicago: University of Chicago Press, 1942.

INDEX

INDEX